THIRD EDITION

FLASHMAPS
BOSTON

Editorial Updater
Chris Billy

Cartographic Updater
Marcy Pritchard

Proofreader
Andrew Collins

Editor
Robert Blake

Cover Design
Guido Caroti

Creative Director
Fabrizio La Rocca

Cartographer
David Lindroth

Designer
Tigist Getachew

Cartographic Contributors
Edward Faherty
Tim Faherty
Page Lindroth
Dan Neumann
Eric Rudolph

Fodor's

www.fodors.com

Fodor's Travel Publications · New York, Toronto, London, S

Contents

JUL 2003

ESSENTIAL INFORMATION	**MAP**
Important Telephone Numbers	iv–vi
The New England Coast	1
Eastern Massachusetts	2
Boston Area	3
Streetfinder/Downtown Boston	4
Streetfinder/Cambridge	5
Zip Codes	6
Neighborhoods	7
Hospitals/Boston Area	8
Hospitals/Longwood Medical Area	9
Consulates & Missions	10
Libraries	11
Universities, Colleges & Schools	12
Universities & Colleges/Boston Area	13
Harvard and Radcliffe	14
Massachusetts Institute of Technology	15
Boston University	16

TRANSPORTATION	**MAP**
Logan International Airport	17
Driving & Parking/Downtown	18
MBTA Rapid Transit/Downtown	19
MBTA Rapid Transit/Boston Area	20
Buses/Downtown	21
Buses/Boston Area	22
Commuter Rail Lines & Outer T Stops	23

EXPLORING	**MAP**
Top Attractions	24
Freedom Trail & Black Heritage Trail	25
Architecture	26
Outdoor Statuary	27
Churches and Cemeteries	28
Museum of Fine Arts	29
Museums	30
Art Galleries/Newbury Street	31
Exploring Cambridge	32
Exploring Lexington	33

3 9082 08880 8376

EXPLORING (cont.)

	MAP
Exploring Salem	34
Exploring Concord	35
Exploring Cape Ann	36

PARKS & RECREATION

	MAP
Parks & Recreation	37
The Emerald Necklace	38
Beaches	39
Martha's Vineyard & Nantucket	40
Stadiums & Arenas	41

SHOPPING

	MAP
Shopping/Back Bay	42
Shopping/Beacon Hill & Downtown	43
Shopping/Cambridge	44
Shopping Centers/Boston Area	45

RESTAURANTS & HOTELS

	MAP
Restaurants/Downtown	46
Restaurants/Cambridge	47
Restaurants/Salem	48
Restaurants/Cape Ann	49
Hotels/Greater Boston	50
Hotels/Downtown	51

NIGHTLIFE

	MAP
Performing Arts/Cambridge	52
Performing Arts/Downtown	53
Movies	54
Nightlife/Cambridge & Somerville	55
Nightlife/Boston	56

Special Sales

Fodor's Travel Publications are available at special discounts for bulk purchases for sales promotions or premiums. Special editions, including personalized covers, excerpts of existing guides, and corporate imprints, can be created in large quantities for special needs. For more information, contact your local bookseller or write to Special Markets, Fodor's Travel Publications, 280 Park Avenue, New York, NY 10017. Inquiries from Canada should be directed to your local Canadian bookseller or sent to Random House of Canada, Ltd., Marketing Dept., 2775 Matheson Blvd. East, Mississauga, Ontario L4W4P7. Inquiries from the United Kingdom should be sent to Fodor's Travel Publications, 20 Vauxhall Bridge Rd., London, SW1V 2SA, England. **ISBN 0-679-00786-5**   **ISSN 1533-2233**

PRINTED IN GERMANY 10 9 8 7 6 5 4 3 2 1

Area Codes: All (617) unless otherwise noted.

EMERGENCIES

Ambulance/Fire/Police ☎ 911

Animal Emergency ☎ 522-7282

Animal Rescue League ☎ 426-9170

Animal Shelter (MSPCA)
☎ 522-5055

Battered Women's Hotline
☎ 661-7203

Child-at-Risk Hotline
☎ 800/792-5200

Children's Aid ☎ 267-3700

Coast Guard ☎ 565-9200

Dental Emergencies & Referrals
☎ 636-6828, 800/917-6453

Drug & Alcohol Hotlines
☎ 445-1500, 624-5111, 800/327-5050

Parental Stress Hotline
☎ 800/632-8188

Poison Information Center
☎ 232-2120, 800/682-9211

Rape Crisis Center
☎ 492-7273

Suicide Prevention ☎ 247-0220

Traveler's Aid ☎ 542-7286, 737-2880

24-hour Pharmacy
☎ 876-5519, 282-5246

Visiting Nurse Assn
☎ 800/696-3838

SERVICES

AAA ☎ 800/222-4357

AARP ☎ 723-7600

AIDS Hotline ☎ 800/235-2331

Alcoholics Anonymous ☎ 426-9444

Amex Lost Charge Cards
☎ 800/528-4800

Amex Lost Travelers Checks
☎ 800/221-7282

Attorney General ☎ 727-2200

Better Business Bureau ☎ 426-9000

Birth Certificates ☎ 635-4177

**Black Community Information
Center** ☎ 445-3098

Broken Streetlights ☎ 635-7500

Chamber of Commerce ☎ 227-4500

Citizens Info Service ☎ 727-7030

City Hall Boston ☎ 635-4000

City Hall Cambridge ☎ 349-4000

Consumer Affairs ☎ 727-7780

Convention & Visitors Bureau
☎ 536-4100

Federal Bureau of Investigation
☎ 742-5533

Garbage Collection ☎ 635-7573

Governor's Office ☎ 727-3600

Handicapped Information
☎ 727-7440, 800/642-0249

Immigration ☎ 565-3879

Internal Revenue Service
☎ 800/829-3676

Legal Advice or Referrals
☎ 742-9179

Library/Boston Public ☎ 536-5400

**Mass Commission Against
Discrimination** ☎ 727-3990

**Mass Turnpike Road/Weather
Conditions** ☎ 800/828-9104

Mayor's Office ☎ 635-4000

Medicaid
☎ 348-5500, 800/841-2900

Medicare
☎ 800/882-1228

Parking Tickets ☎ 635-4410

Passports ☎ 565-6990

Physician Referral ☎ 726-5800

Planned Parenthood ☎ 616-1616,
800/682-9218

Postal Service ☎ 654-5001,
654-5083

Public Health ☎ 624-6000

Registry of Motor Vehicles
☎ 351-4500

Snow Removal Boston: ☎ 635-3050,
Cambridge: ☎ 349-4860

Social Security ☎ 800/772-1213

State Police ☎ 508/820-2300

Time of Day ☎ 637-1234, 637-1111

Towaways ☎ 635-3900

Traffic/Road Reports
☎ 374-1234

Travel & Tourism
☎ 727-3201, 800/447-6277

Veteran's Administration
☎ 800/827-1000

Weather ☎ 936-1234

Zip Code Info ☎ 654-7567

Area Codes: All (617) unless otherwise noted.

TOURS

Cruises

A C Cruise Line ☎ 261-6633

Bay State Cruise Co ☎ 723-8012

Boston Harbor Cruises ☎ 227-4320

Boston Harbor Whale Watch
☎ 345-9866

Charles River Boat Co ☎ 621-3001

Mass Bay Lines ☎ 542-8000

New England Aquarium ☎ 973-5281

Odyssey Cruises ☎ 654-9700

Spirit of Boston ☎ 748-1450

Sightseeing

Arlington Street Church ☎ 536-7050

Bay Colony Historical Tours
☎ 523-7303

Beacon Hill Gardens ☎ 227-4392

Beantown Trolley ☎ 781/986-6100

Boston By Foot ☎ 367-2345

Boston Duck Tours ☎ 723-3825

Boston Globe ☎ 929-2653

Boston Public Library ☎ 536-5400

Brush Hill Tours ☎ 781/986-6100

Christian Science Center
☎ 450-3790

Discovering Boston ☎ 323-2554

Federal Reserve Bank ☎ 973-3451

Freedom Trail Tours
☎ 242-5642

Gray Lines ☎ 781/986-6100

Historic Boston ☎ 227-4679

Historic Neighborhoods ☎ 426-1885

John Hancock Observatory
☎ 247-1977

Mass Bay Brewing Co ☎ 574-9551

Minuteman Tours ☎ 876-5539

Old State House ☎ 242-5642

Old Town Trolley ☎ 269-7010

Skywalk ☎ 859-0648

Trinity Church ☎ 536-0944

USS *Constitution* ☎ 426-1812

Victorian Society ☎ 267-6338

Whites of Their Eyes ☎ 241-7575

Women's Heritage Trails
☎ 242-5642

TRANSPORTATION

Amtrak ☎ 800/872-7245; 482-3660

Bonanza Bus Terminal ☎ 720-4110

Boston Cab ☎ 262-2227

Boston Cab Assn ☎ 536-5010

Cambridge Cab ☎ 354-5005

Ferries:

    Bay State Cruise Company
    Boston to Hull or Provincetown
    ☎ 723-8012

    Hy-Line Ferries
    Hyannis to Martha's Vineyard or
    Nantucket ☎ 508/778-2600

    Massachusetts Bay Lines
    Boston to Hingham ☎ 542-8000

    Steamship Authority
    Woods Hole to Martha's Vineyard
    ☎ 508/477-8600
    Hyannis to Nantucket
    ☎ 508/771-4000, 508/477-8600

Greyhound Bus Terminal
☎ 526-1801, 800/231-2222

**Independent Taxi Operators
Assoc** ☎ 268-1313

**Logan Airport Ground
Transportation** ☎ 800/235-6426

Logan International Airport
☎ 567-5400

Logan Water Shuttle ☎ 330-8680

**Mass Bay Transportation Authority
(MBTA: Bus, 'T', Commuter Rail)**
☎ 222-3200, 800/392-6100

**MBTA Hearing Impaired
Information** ☎ 222-5415

MBTA Logan Airport
☎ 800/235-6426

MBTA Lost & Found ☎ 222-3200

MBTA Police ☎ 222-1212

MBTA Road Conditions/Weather
☎ 800/828-9104

MBTA Special Needs ☎ 222-5123

Metro Cab ☎ 242-8000

Peter Pan Bus Lines
☎ 800/343-9999

PARKS AND RECREATION

Arnold Arboretum ☎ 524-1717

Beaches ☎ 727-5114

Bicycling ☎ 542-2453

Boating ☎ 227-4198

Fishing ☎ 727-3151

Golf Courses:

George Wright, Hyde Park
☎ 361-8313

William Devine, Dorchester
☎ 265-4084

Fresh Pond, Cambridge
☎ 349- 6282

Newton Commonwealth,
Newton ☎ 630-1971

Ice Skating ☎ 727-5114

In-Line Skating (rentals)
☎ 482-7400

**Metropolitan District Commission
(MDC)** ☎ 727-5114

Parks & Recreation Info
☎ 635-4505

Racket Sports ☎ 482-8881

**Running: Boston Athletic Assoc
(Boston Marathon)** ☎ 236-1652

Skiing:

Blue Hills ☎ 698-1802
(downhill)

Middlesex Fells Reservation,
Stoneham ☎ 781/662-5214
(cross-country)

Swimming ☎ 727-5114

YMCA ☎ 536-7800

YWCA ☎ 351-7600

SPECTATOR SPORTS

Boston Bruins/Hockey ☎ 624-1900

Boston Celtics/Basketball
☎ 523-3030

Boston Marathon ☎ 236-1652

Boston Red Sox/Baseball
☎ 267-8661

Dog Racing/Wonderland
☎ 781/284-1300

Horse Racing/Suffolk Downs
☎ 567-3900

LPGA/Blue Hills CC ☎ 781/828-2000

New England Patriots/Football
☎ 800/543-1776

PGA/Pleasant Valley CC
☎ 508/865-4441

Polo/Myopia Hunt Club
☎ 978/468-4433

Tennis/US Pro Longwood
☎ 731-2900

INTERCOLLEGIATE ATHLETICS

Babson ☎ 781/239-4250

Boston College ☎ 552-3000

Boston University ☎ 353-4632

Brandeis ☎ 781/736-3630

Harvard ☎ 495-4848

MIT ☎ 253-4498

Northeastern ☎ 373-2672

Tufts ☎ 627-3232

ENTERTAINMENT

Berklee Performance Center
☎ 266-7455

BOSTIX ☎ 723-5181

Boston Ballet ☎ 695-6950

Boston Camerata ☎ 262-2092

Boston Lyric Opera ☎ 542-4912

Boston Pops ☎ 266-1492

Boston Symphony Orchestra
☎ 266-1492

Children's Museum ☎ 426-6500

Colonial Theatre ☎ 426-9366

Dance Umbrella Inc ☎ 482-7570

Fleet Boston Celebrity Series
☎ 482-2595

FleetCenter ☎ 624-1000

Franklin Park Zoo/Stone Zoo
☎ 442-2002

Handel & Haydn Society
☎ 266-3605

Harborfest (summer) ☎ 227-1528

Hub Ticket Agency ☎ 426-8340

Movie Fone ☎ 333-3456

Museum of Fine Arts ☎ 267-9300

Museum of Science ☎ 723-2500

New England Aquarium
☎ 973-5200

New England Conservatory
☎ 536-2412

Orpheum Theatre ☎ 679-0810

Sanders Theatre/Harvard
☎ 496-2222

Shubert Theatre ☎ 482-9393

Symphony Hall ☎ 266-1492

Ticketmaster ☎ 931-2000

**Tweeter Center for the Performing
Arts** ☎ 508/339-2333

Wang Center ☎ 482-9393

Wilbur Theatre ☎ 423-4008

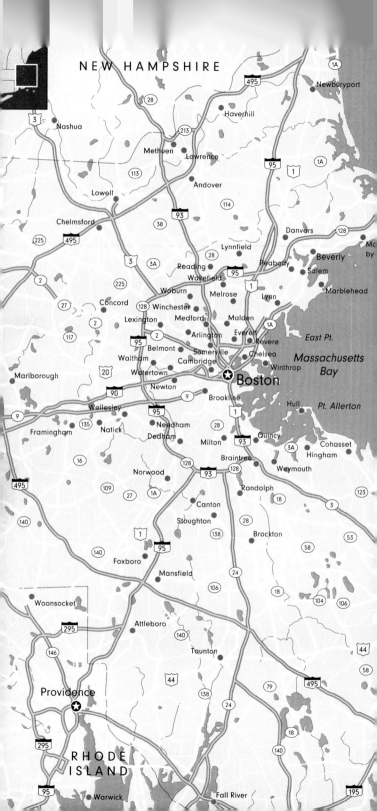

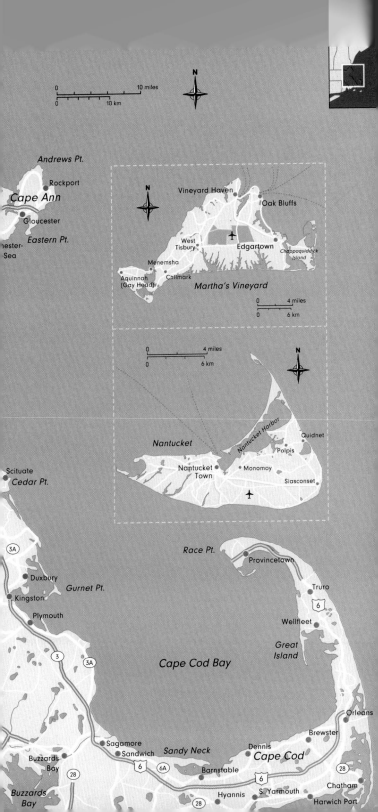

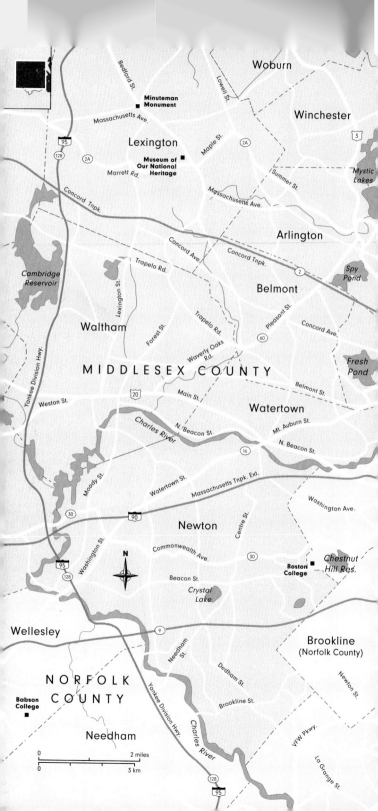

MAP 4 Streetfinder/Downtown Boston

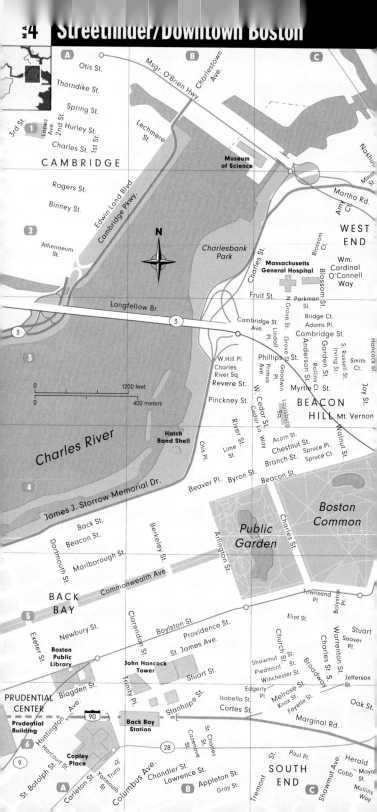

A   B   C

Otis St.

Thorndike St.

Spring St.

Msgr. O'Brien Hwy.

Charlestown Ave.

Nashua

3rd St.

Lopez Ave.

2nd Hurley St.

1st St.

Charles St.

Lechmere St.

Minor St.

1 CAMBRIDGE

Museum of Science

Rogers St.

Binney St.

Edwin Land Blvd.

Cambridge Pkwy.

Martha Rd.

Amp

WEST END

2 Athenaeum St.

N

Charlesbank Park

Charles St.

Blossom Ct.

Wm. Cardinal O'Connell Way

Massachusetts General Hospital

Fruit St.

Grove St.

Blossom St.

Parkman St.

Bridge Ct.

Adams Pl.

Hancock St.

Longfellow Br.

3

Cambridge St. Ave.

Cambridge St.

Garden St.

S. Russell St.

Irving St.

Smith Ct.

3

W. Hill Pl.

Charles River Sq.

Lindall

Phillips St.

Grove St.

Goodwin

Anderson St.

Rollins Ct.

St.

Joy St.

Charles River

Revere St.

Primus Ave.

Pinckney St.

W. Cedar St.

Louisburg Sq.

Myrtle St.

BEACON HILL

Mt. Vernon

1200 feet

400 meters

Hatch Band Shell

River St.

W. Cedar La Way

Acorn St.

Chestnut St.

Spruce Pl.

Walnut St.

4

James J. Storrow Memorial Dr.

Otis Pl.

Lime St.

Branch St.

Spruce Ct.

Beaver Pl.

Byron St.

Beacon St.

Back St.

Beacon St.

Charles St.

Boston Common

Marlborough St.

Berkeley St.

Public Garden

BACK BAY

Commonwealth Ave.

Arlington St.

Townsend Pl.

Boylston

5

Dartmouth St.

Exeter St.

Newbury St.

Clarendon St.

Boylston St.

Providence St.

St. James Ave.

Eliot St.

Church St.

Warren St.

Stuart

Seaver St.

Boston Public Library

John Hancock Tower

Trinity Pl.

Stuart St.

Shawmut St.

Piedmont St.

Winchester St.

Broadway

Charles St. S.

Jefferson St.

PRUDENTIAL CENTER

Blagden St.

Huntington Ave.

90

Stanhope St.

Edgerly Pl.

Melrose St.

Knox St.

Fayette St.

Oak St.

6

Prudential Building

Harcourt St.

Back Bay Station

Isabella St.

Cortes St.

Marginal Rd.

9

Copley Place

St. Botolph St.

Carleton St.

Yarmouth St.

Truro St.

Columbus Ave.

28

Chandler St.

Lawrence St.

Gray St.

St. Charles St.

Cazenove St.

Appleton St.

Tremont St.

Paul Pl.

Shawmut Ave.

Cobb St.

Herald St.

Mayo St.

Mullins Way

SOUTH END

A   B   C

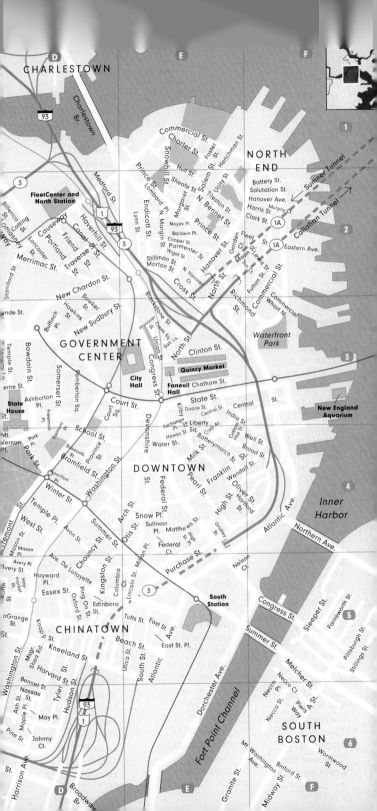

Letter codes refer to grid sectors on preceding map

A St. E6, F5
Acorn St. C4
Adams Pl. C3
Amy Ct. C2
Anderson St. C3
Appleton St. A6, C6
Arch St. D4, E4
Arlington St. B4, C6
Ash St. D5, D6
Ashburton Pl. D3
Atlantic Ave. E5, F2
Ave. De Lafayette D4, D5
Avery Pl. D5
Avery St. D5
Avon St. D4
Back St. A5, B4
Baldwin Pl. E2
Battery St. F2
Batterymarch St. E4
Beach St. D5, E5
Beacon St. A5, D3
Beaver Pl. B4
Bennet St. D5, D6
Berkeley St. B4, B6
Billerica St. D2
Binford St. F6
Blackstone St. D2, E3
Blagden St. A5, A6
Blossom Ct. C2
Blossom St. C2, C3
Bosworth St. D4
Bowdoin St. D3
Bowker St. D2, D3
Boylston Pl. C5
Boylston St. A6, C5
Branch St. C4
Bridge Ct. C3
Brimmer St. B3, B4
Broad St. E4, F4
Broadway C5, C6
Broadway Bridge D6
Bromfield St. D4
Buckingham St. B6
Bulfinch Pl. D3
Byron St. B4, C4
Callahan Tunnel E2, F1
Cambridge St. Ave. B3, C3
Cambridge St. B3, D3
Canal St. D2
Carleton St. A6
Causeway D2, E1
Cazenove St. B6

Cedar Lane Way B3, C4
Central St. E3, F3
Chandler St. B6, C6
Charles River Sq. B3
Charles St. C2, C5
Charles St. S. C5, C6
Charlestown Bridge D1
Charter St. E1, E2
Chatham St. E3
Chauncy St. D4, D5
Chestnut St. B4, C4
Church St. C5, C6
Clarendon St. A4, B6
Clark St. F2
Clinton St. E3
Cobb St. C6
Columbia Ct. D5
Columbus Ave. A6, C5
Commercial St. E1, E3
Commercial Wharf N. F2, F3
Commonwealth Ave. A5, B4
Congress St. E3, F6
Cooper St. E2
Cortes St. B6, C6
Cotting St. D2
Court Sq. D3, D4
Court St. D3, E3
Crab Al. E4
Creek Sq. E3
Cross St. E2, E3
Custom House St. E4
Dartmouth St. A4, B6
Derne St. D3
Devonshire St. E3, E4
Doane St. E3
Dorchester Ave. E6, F4
East St. E5
East St. Pl. E5
Eastern Ave. F2
Edgerly Pl. C5, C6
Edinboro St. D5
Endicott St. E2
Essex St. C5, E5
Exchange Pl. E3, E4
Exeter St. A5, A6
Farnsworth St. F5
Fayette St. C5, C6
Federal Ct. E4
Federal St. E4, E5
Fleet St. E2, F2
Foster St. E1

Franklin St. D4, F4
Freeman Pl. D3
Friend St. D2
Fruit St. B2, C2
Fulton St. E2, F2
Garden Ct. E2
Garden St. C3
Garrison St. A6
Goodwin Pl. C3
Granite St. E6
Gray St. B6
Gridley St. E4
Grove St. C3
Hamilton Pl. D4
Hancock St. C3, D3
Hanover Ave. F2
Hanover St. E3, F1
Harcourt St. A6
Harris St. F2
Harrison Ave. C6, D5
Hartford St. E4, F4
Harvard St. D5
Haverhill St. D2, E2
Hawes St. E4
Hawkins St. D3
Haymarket Pl. D5
Hayward Pl. D5
Henchman St. E1
Herald St. C6, D6
High St. E5, F4
High St. Pl. E4
Hudson St. D5, D6
Hull St. E1, E2
Huntington Ave. A6
India St. E3, F4
Irving St. C3
Isabella St. B6, C6
James J. Storrow Memorial Dr. A4, B4
Jefferson St. C6
Johnny Ct. D6
Joy Pl. C4, D4
Joy St. C3, C4
Kilby St. E3, E4
Kingston St. D4, D5
Knapp St. D5
Kneeland St. D5, E5
LaGrange St. C5, D5
Lancaster St. D2
Lawrence St. B6
Lewis St. F2
Liberty Sq. E4
Lincoln St. D5, E5

Letter codes refer to grid sectors on preceding map

Lindall Pl. C3
Lomasney Way C2, D2
Lombard Pl. E2
Longfellow Br. A3, B3
Louisburg Sq. C3, C4
Lynde St. D3
Lynn St. E2
Maple Pl. D6
Margaret St. E2
Marginal Rd. C6, D6
Marlborough St. A5, B5
Martha Rd. C2, D2
Mason Pl. D4
Mason St. D4, D5
Matthews St. E4
May Pl. D6
Mayo St. C6
Medford St. D2
Melcher St. F5, F6
Melrose St. C5, C6
Merrimac St. D2
Midway St. F6
Milk St. D4, F3
Milton Pl. E4, E5
Minot St. C2
Moon St. E2, F2
Morton St. E2
Msgr. Shea Rd. D5
Mt. Vernon Pl. C3
Mt. Vernon St. B4, D3
Mt. Washington Ave. E6, F6
Murphy Ct. F2
Myrtle St. C3
N. Bennet St. E2
N. Grove St. C3
N. Hanover Ct. E2
N. Margin St. E2
N. Washington St. D1, E2
Nashua St. C1, D2
Nassau St. D6
Necco Ct. F5, F6
Necco Pl. F5, F6
Necco St. F6
Nelson Ct. E5
New Chardon St. D3, E2
New Sudbury St. D3, E2
Newbury St. A5, B5
North St. E3, F2
Northern Ave. F4, F5
Noyes Pl. E2

Oak St. D6
Oliver St. E4, F4
Otis Pl. B4
Otis St. E4
Oxford St. D5
Park Pl. D4
Park St. D4
Parkman St. C3
Parmenter St. E2
Paul Pl. C6
Pearl St. E4
Pemberton Sq. D3
Phillips St. C3
Piedmont St. C5
Pinckney St. B3, C3
Pine St. D6
Ping On St. D5
Pittsburgh St. F5
Portland St. D2
Primus Ave. C3
Prince St. E1, E2
Providence St. B5, C5
Province St. D4
Purchase St. D5, F4
Revere St. B3, C3
Richmond St. E2, F3
Ridgeway La. D3
River St. B3, C4
Rollins Ct. C3
S. Russell St. C3
Salem St. E1, E2
Salt La. E3
Salutation St. F2
School St. D3, E4
Shawmut Ave. C6, D5
Shawmut St. C6
Sheafe St. E2
Sleeper St. F5
Smith Ct. C3
Snow Pl. E4
Snowhill St. E1, E2
Somerset St. D3
South St. E5
Spruce Ct. C4
Spruce Pl. C4
St. Botolph St. A6
St. Charles St. B6
St. James Ave. A5, B5
Stanhope St. B6
Staniford St. D2, D3
State St. E3, F3
Stillings St. F5
Stillman St. E2

Stuart St. A6, D5
Sullivan Pl. E4
Summer St. D4, E5
Sumner Tunnel E2, F1
Sun Ct. E2, F2
Tamworth St. D5
Temple Pl. D4
Temple St. D3
Tileston St. E2
Townsend Pl. C5
Traverse St. D2
Tremont Pl. D3, D4
Tremont St. B6, D3
Trinity Pl. B5, B6
Truro St. A6
Tufts St. E5
Tyler St. D5, D6
Union St. E3
Unity St. E2
Utica St. E5
W. Cedar St. C3, D3
W. Hill Pl. B3
Walnut St. C3, C4
Warrenton St. C5
Washington St. C6, E3
Water St. E4
Well St. E4, F4
Wendell St. E4, F4
West St. D4
Wiget St. E2
Winchester St. C5
Winter St. D4
Wm. Cardinal O'Connell Way C2, D2
Wm. E. Mullins Way C6, D6
Wormwood St. F6
Yarmouth St. A6

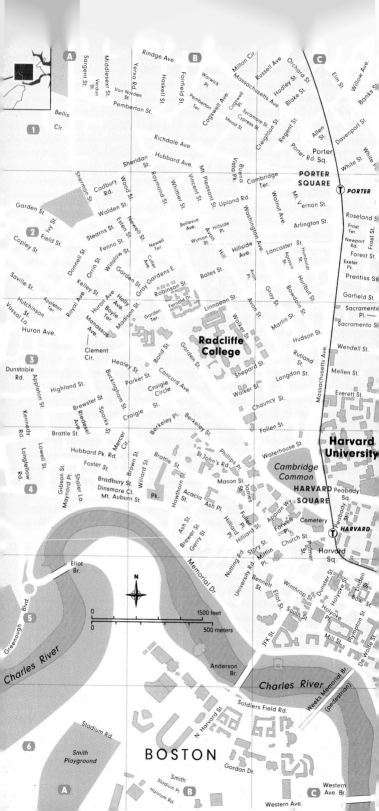

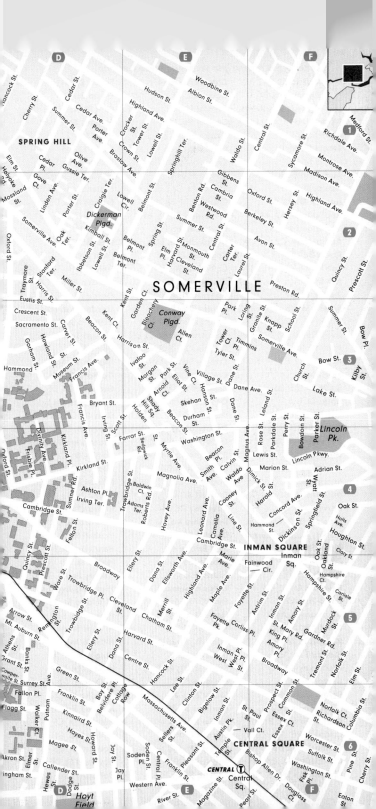

Letter codes refer to grid sectors on preceding map

Acacia St. B4
Adams Ter. E4
Agassiz St. C2
Akron St. D6
Allen St. C1
Amory Pl. F5
Amory St. F5
Anderson Bridge B6
Antrim St. E5, F5
Appian Way C4
Appleton St. A2, A4
Appleton Ter. A3
Arlington St. C2
Arrow St. D5
Ash Pl. B4
Ash St. B4
Ashton Pl. D4
Athens St. D5
Austin Pk. E6
Avon Hill St. B2
Avon Pl. B2, C2
Avon St. B2, C3
Baldwin Ct. E4
Banks St. D5, D6
Bates St. B2
Bay St. D5, D6
Beech St. C1
Bellevue Ave. B2
Bellis Cir. A1
Belvidere Pl. D6
Bennett St. B5, C5
Berkeley Pl. B3, B4
Berkeley St. B3, B4
Bigelow St. E5, E6
Bishop Allen Dr. E6, F6
Blake St. C1
Bond St. B3
Bow St. C5, D5
Bowdoin St. C2, C3
Boyle Ter. A3
Bradbury St. A4
Brattle St. A3, C4
Brewer St. B4
Brewster St. A3
Broadway D4, F6
Brown St. B4
Bryant St. D3, E3
Buckingham St. A3
Buena Vista Pk. B1, B2
Cadbury Rd. A1
Callender St. D6
Cambridge St. C4, F5
Cambridge Ter. B2, C2

Camelia Ave. E4
Carver St. D3
Central Pl. E6
Central Sq. E6
Centre St. D5, E5
Chatham St. E5
Chauncy St. B3, C3
Cherry St. F6
Church St. C4
Clary St. F4, F5
Cleveland St. D5, E5
Clinton St. E5, E6
Cogswell Ave. B1
Cogswell Pl. B1
Columbia St. F5, F6
Common St. F5, F6
Concord Ave. A2, C4
Copley St. A2
Cottage Row D6
Cowperthwaite St. C6, D6
Craigie Cir. B3
Craigie St. A3, B3
Creighton St. C1
Crescent St. D3
Cypress St. B1
Dana St. D5, E4
Davenport St. C1
De Wolfe St. C5, D5
Dinsmore Ct. A4, B4
Divinity Ave. D3, D4
Dodge St. D6
Donnell St. A2
Douglass Ct. F6
Dunstable Rd. A3
Dunster St. C5
Eliot Bridge A5
Eliot St. C5
Ellery St. D5, E4
Ellsworth Ave. E4, E5
Elm St. F5, F6
Elmer St. D6
Essex Ct. F6
Essex St. E6, F6
Esten St. A2, B2
Eustis St. D2, E3
Everett St. C3
Exeter Pk. C2
Fairfield St. B1
Fallon Pl. D6
Farrar St. D4, E3
Farwell Pl. C4
Fayette Pk. E5
Fayette St. E5, F5

Felton St. D4
Fenno St. A2
Fern St. A2
Fernald Dr. B2, B3
Field St. A2
Flagg St. D6
Follen St. B4, C3
Forest St. C2, D2
Foster St. A4, B4
Francis Ave. D3, D4
Franklin St. D6, E6
Frisbie Pl. D4
Frost St. C2
Frost Ter. C2
Fuller Pl. B4
Garden St. A2, C4
Garden Ter. B3
Gardner Rd. F5
Garfield St. C2, D2
Gerard Ter. C2, D2
Gerry St. B4
Gibson St. A4
Gorham St. D3
Grant St. C5, D5
Gray Gardens E. B2
Gray St. C2, C3
Green St. D5, F6
Greenough Blvd. A5
Hadley St. C1
Hammond St. D3
Hancock St. D6, E5
Harris St. D2, D3
Harvard Sq. C4, C5
Harvard St. D5, F6
Haskell St. B1
Hawthorn St. B4
Hayes St. D6
Healey St. A3, B3
Highland Ave. E4, E5
Highland St. A3
Hilliard Pl. B4
Hilliard St. B4, C4
Hillside Ave. B2, C2
Hingham St. D6
Holden St. E3, E4
Holly Ave. A2, A3
Holyoke Pl. C5
Holyoke Rd. D1
Holyoke St. C5
Hovey Ave. E4
Howard St. D6
Howland St. D3
Hubbard Ave. B1

Hubbard Park Rd. A4
Hudson St. C3
Humboldt St. C2
Hurlbut St. C2, C3
Huron Ave. A3, B2
Hutchinson St. A3
Inman Pl. E5
Inman Sq. F4, F5
Inman St. E6, F5
Irving St. D3, D4
Irving Ter. D4
Ivy St. A2
James St. B4
Jay Pl. D6, E6
Jay St. D6
JFK St. B5, C5
Kelley St. A2
Kennedy Rd. A3, A4
King Pl. F5
Kinnaird St. D6, E6
Kirkland Pl. D4
Kirkland St. D4, E4
Lancaster St. C2
Langdon St. C3
Lee St. E5, E6
Leonard Ave. E4
Linden St. C5
Linnaean St. B3, C2
Longfellow Rd. A4
Lowell St. A4
Madison St. A3, B2
Magazine St. E6
Magee St. D6
Magnolia Ave. E4
Manassas Ave. A3
Maple Ave. E4, E5
Marie Ave. E4, E5
Martin St. C3
Mason St. B4, C4
Massachusetts
Ave. B1, F6
Maynard Pl. A4
Mead St. B1
Mellen St. C3
Memorial Dr. A4, D6
Mercer Cir. A4
Merrill St. E5
Middlesex St. A1
Mifflin Pl. C4, C5
Mill St. C5, D5
Mt. Auburn St. A4, D5
Mt. Pleasant St. B1, B2
Mt. Vernon St. C2

Murdock St. F5
Museum St. D3
Myrtle Ave. E4
Newell St. A2, B2
Newport Rd. C2
Norfolk Ct. F6
Norfolk St. F5, F6
Nutting Rd. B4, B5
Oakland St. F4, F5
Orchard St. C1
Orrin St. A2
Oxford St. D2, D4
Palmer St. C4, C5
Parker St. A3, B3
Peabody Sq. C4
Peabody St. C4
Pearl St. E6, F6
Pemberton St. A1, B1
Pemberton Ter. B1
Phillips Pl. B4
Pine St. F6
Pleasant St. E6
Plympton St. C5
Porter Rd. C1
Porter Sq. C1
Prentiss St. C2, D2
Prescott St. D4, D5
Prospect St. E6, F4
Putnam Ave. D5, D6
Quincy St. D4, D5
Raymond St. B1, B3
Regent St. C1
Remington St. D5
Richardson St. F6
Richdale Ave. B1, C2
Riedesel Ave. A3, A4
Rindge Ave. A1, B1
River St. D6, E6
Roberts Rd. E4
Robinson St. B2
Roseland St. C2, D2
Royal Ave. A3
Russell Ave. B1, C1
Rutland St. C3
Sacramento Pl. C3
Sacramento St. C3, D3
St. John's Rd. B4
St. Mary Rd. F5
St. Paul St. E6, F6
Sargent St. A1
Saville St. A2, A3
Scott St. D4, E3

Sedgwick Rd. E4
Sellers St. E6
Shady Hill Sq. E3
Shaler La. A4
Shepard St. B3, C3
Sheridan St. B1
Sherman St. A1, A2
Soden Pl. E6
Soden St. E6
Soldiers Field Rd. A4, C6
South St. C5
Sparks St. A3, A4
Stearns St. A2
Story St. B4, C4
Suffolk St. F6
Sumner Rd. D4
Surrey St. D5
Sycamore St. B1
Temple St. E6
Traymore St. D2
Tremont St. F4, F5
Trowbridge Pl. D5
Trowbridge St. D5, E4
University Rd. B5
Upland Rd. B2, C2
Vail Ct. E6
Van Norden St. A1, B1
Vassal La. A2, A3
Verdun St. A1
Vincent St. B2
Walden St. A3, B1
Walker Ct. D6
Walker St. B3, C3
Walnut Ave. C2
Ware St. D4, D5
Warwick Pl. B1
Washington Ave. B2, C2
Washington St. F6
Waterhouse St. C4
Wendell St. C3, D3
West Pl. E5
West St. E5
Western Ave. A6, E6
Western Ave. Br. C6
White Pl. C1
White St. C1
Whittier St. B1
Willard St. B4
Winslow St. A2, B2
Winthrop St. C5
Wood St. A1, A2
Worcester St. F6
Yerxa Rd. B1

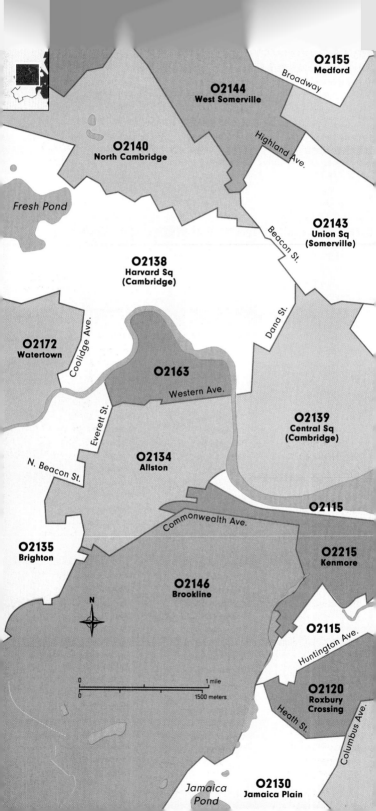

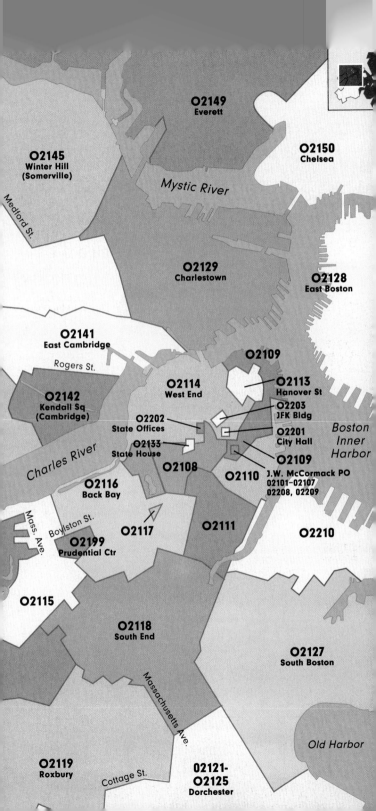

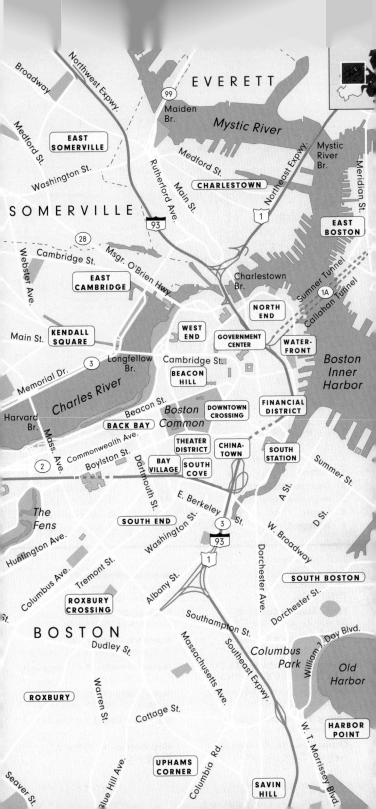

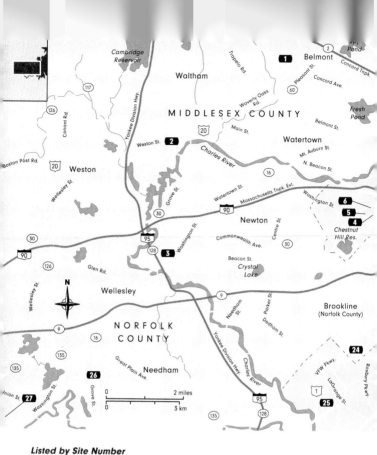

Listed by Site Number

1	McLean	**6**	Franciscan Children's	**10**	Youville
2	Deaconess Waltham			**11**	Cambridge
3	Newton-Wellesley	**7**	St John of God	**12**	Mass Eye & Ear
4	Vencor	**8**	Mt Auburn	**13**	Mass General
5	St Elizabeth's	**9**	Somerville	**14**	Shriner's Hospital

Listed Alphabetically

Arbour Psychiatric, 20.
49 Robinwood Ave, Jamaica Plain
☎ 522-4400

Boston Medical Center, 18.
818 Harrison Ave ☎ 534-5000

Boston U Medical Center, 17.
88 E Newton St ☎ 638-8000

Bournewood Psychiatric, 24. 300
South St, Brookline ☎ 469-0300

Cambridge, 11. 1493 Cambridge St,
Cambridge ☎ 665-1000

Carney, 22. 2100 Dorchester Ave,
Dorchester ☎ 296-4000

Charles River, 26. 203 Grove St,
Wellesley ☎ 781/416-5300

Deaconess Waltham, 2.
Hope Ave, Waltham
☎ 781/647-6000

Faulkner, 23. 1153 Centre St,
Jamaica Plain ☎ 983-7000

Franciscan Children's, 6.
30 Warren St, Brighton ☎ 254-3800

Jewish Memorial, 19. 59 Townsend St
☎ 442-8760

Lemuel Shattuck, 21. 170 Morton St,
Jamaica Plain ☎ 522-8110

Mass Eye & Ear, 12. 243 Charles St
☎ 523-7900

Mass General, 13. 55 Fruit St
☎ 726-2000

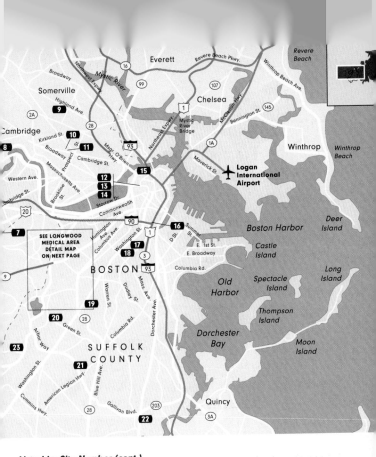

Listed by Site Number (cont.)

- **15** Spaulding Rehab
- **16** New Eng Medical Center
- **17** BU Med Center
- **18** Boston Medical Ctr
- **19** Jewish Memorial
- **20** Arbour Psychiatric
- **21** Lemuel Shattuck
- **22** Carney
- **23** Faulkner
- **24** Bournewood Psychiatric
- **25** VA-Med Center
- **26** Charles River
- **27** Metrowest Med Ctr

Listed Alphabetically (cont.)

McLean, 1. 115 Mill St, Belmont ☎ 855-2000

Metrowest Medical Center, 27. 67 Union St, Natick ☎ 508/650-7000

Mt Auburn, 8. 330 Mt Auburn St, Cambridge ☎ 492-3500

New England Med Center, 16. 750 Washington St ☎ 636-5000

Newton-Wellesley, 3. 2014 Washington St, Newton ☎ 243-6000

St Elizabeth's, 5. 736 Cambridge St, Brighton ☎ 789-3000

St John of God, 7. 296 Allston St, Brighton ☎ 277-5750

Shriner's Hospital for Children, 14. 51 Blossom St ☎ 722-3000

Somerville, 9. 230 Highland Ave, Somerville ☎ 666-4400

Spaulding Rehabilitation, 15. 125 Nashua St ☎ 573-7000

VA-Med Center, 25. 1400 VFW Pkwy, W Roxbury ☎ 323-7700

Vencor, 4. 1515 Commonwealth Ave, Brighton ☎ 254-1100

Youville, 10. 1575 Cambridge St, Cambridge ☎ 876-4344

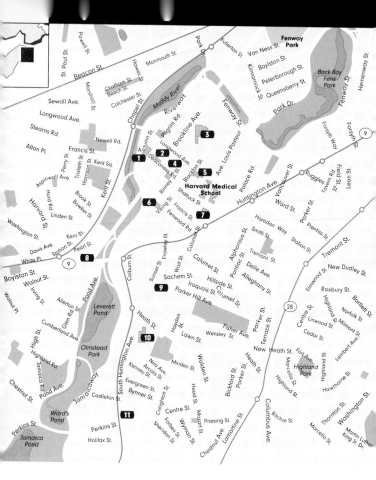

Listed by Site Number

1 Beth Israel Deaconess-West

2 Joslin Diabetes Center

3 Beth Israel Deaconess-East

4 Children's

5 Dana-Farber Cancer Institute

6 Mass Mental Health Center

7 Brigham & Women's

8 Brookline Animal Hospital

9 New England Baptist

10 VA-Med Ctr

11 Angell Memorial Animal Hospital

Listed Alphabetically

Angell Memorial Animal Hospital, 11. 350 S Huntington Ave ☎ 522-7282

Beth Israel Deaconess Med Ctr, 3. East Campus: 330 Brookline Ave ☎ 667-7000

Beth Israel Deaconess Med Ctr, 1. West Campus: I Deaconess Rd ☎ 632-7000

Brigham & Women's, 7. 75 Francis St ☎ 732-5500

Brookline Animal Hospital, 8. 678 Brookline Ave ☎ 277-2090

Children's, 4. 300 Longwood Ave ☎ 355-6000

Dana-Farber Cancer Inst, 5. 44 Binney St ☎ 632-3000

Joslin Diabetes Ctr, 2. I Joslin Pl ☎ 732-2400

Mass Mental Health Ctr, 6. 74 Fenwood Rd ☎ 626-9300

New Eng Baptist, 9. 125 Parker Hill Ave ☎ 754-5800

VA-Med Ctr, 10. I50 So Huntington Ave, Jamaica Plain ☎ 232-9500

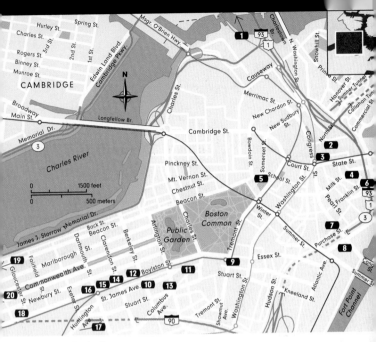

Listed Alphabetically

Australia, 11. 20 Park Plaza
☎ 542-8655

Austria, 5. 15 School St ☎ 227-3131

Belgium, 1. 300 Commercial St,
Malden ☎ 781/397-8566

Brazil, 11. 20 Park Plaza ☎ 542-4000

Canada, 17. 3 Copley Pl ☎ 262-3760

Cape Verde, 16. 607 Boylston St
☎ 353-0014

Chile, 4. 79 Milk St ☎ 232-0416

Colombia, 14. 535 Boylston St
☎ 536-6222

Denmark, 11. 20 Park Plaza
☎ 542-1415

Dominican Rep, 11. 20 Park Plaza
☎ 482-8121

France, 10. 31 St James Ave
☎ 542-7344

Germany, 17. 3 Copley Pl
☎ 536-4414

Great Britain, 8. 600 Atlantic Ave
☎ 248-9555

Greece, 19. 86 Beacon St
☎ 523-0100

Haiti, 15. 545 Boylston St ☎ 266-3660

Hungary, 3. 75 State St ☎ 342-4022

Ireland, 15. 535 Boylston St
☎ 267-9330

Israel, 11. 20 Park Plaza ☎ 542-0041

Italy, 9. 100 Boylston St ☎ 542-0483

Japan, 8. 600 Atlantic Ave
☎ 973-9772

Mexico, 11. 20 Park Plaza
☎ 426-4942

Netherlands, 13. 6 St James Ave
☎ 542-8452

Norway, 7. 286 Congress St
☎ 423-2515

Peru, 14. 535 Boylston St ☎ 388-1144

Poland, 2. 2 Faneuil Hall ☎ 357-1980

Portugal, 18. 899 Boylston St
☎ 536-8740

Republic of Korea, 20.
One Gateway Ctr, Newton
☎ 641-2830

Romania, 6. 85 E India Row
☎ 624-0228

Spain, 15. 545 Boylston St
☎ 536-2506

Sweden, 7. 286 Congress St
☎ 725-0295

Thailand, 12. 20 Park Plaza
☎ 350-6200

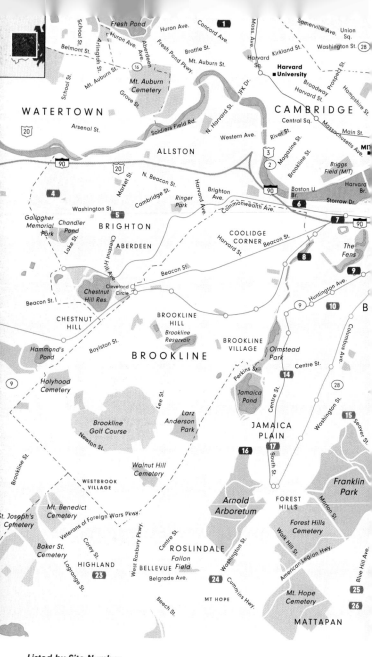

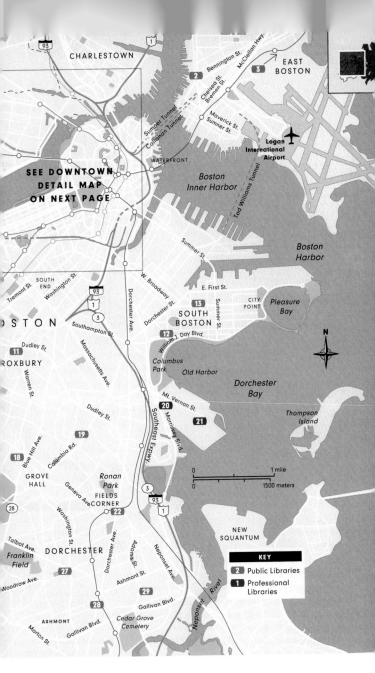

CHARLESTOWN

EAST
BOSTON

Bennington St.
Chelsea St.
Bremen St.
Maverick St.
Sumner St.

Sumner Tunnel
Callahan Tunnel

WATERFRONT

Logan
International
Airport

*Boston
Inner Harbor*

Ted Williams Tunnel

**SEE DOWNTOWN
DETAIL MAP
ON NEXT PAGE**

*Boston
Harbor*

Summer St.

SOUTH
END

Tremont St.
Washington St.

W. Broadway

E. First St.

CITY
POINT

*Pleasure
Bay*

BOSTON

Southampton St.

Dorchester Ave.

Dorchester St.

13 SOUTH
BOSTON

Summer St.

N

11 Dudley St.

ROXBURY

Warren St.

Massachusetts Ave.

12 William J. Day Blvd.

Columbus
Park

Old Harbor

*Dorchester
Bay*

*Thompson
Island*

Dudley St.

19

Mt. Vernon St.

20

Morrissey Blvd.

21

18 Blue Hill Ave.

Columbia Rd.

Southeast Expwy.

GROVE
HALL

*Ronan
Park*

Geneva Ave. FIELDS
CORNER

28

Washington St.

22

0   1 mile
0   1500 meters

Talbot Ave.

*Franklin
Field*

DORCHESTER

Dorchester Ave.

Adams St.

Neponset Ave.

NEW
SQUANTUM

27

Woodrow Ave.

Ashmont St.

29 Gallivan Blvd.

KEY

2 Public Libraries

1 Professional
Libraries

28

ASHMONT

Gallivan Blvd.

*Cedar Grove
Cemetery*

Neponset River

Morton St.

Listed by Site Number (cont.)

17 Jamaica Plain
18 Grove Hall
19 Uphams Corner
20 Boston Globe
    Newspaper

21 Kennedy
    Presidential
22 Fields Corner
23 West Roxbury
24 Roslindale

25 Mattapan
26 Hyde Park
27 Codman Square
28 Lower Mills
29 Adams Street

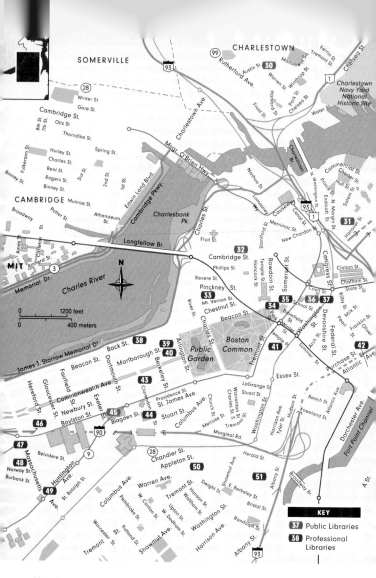

Listed by Site Number

30 Charlestown

31 North End

32 West End

33 Archives of American Art

34 Congregational Library

35 Boston Athenaeum

36 Kirstein Business

37 Bostonian Society

38 Goethe Institute

39 French Library

40 Boston Psychoanalytic

41 Crime & Justice Foundation

42 Federal Reserve Bank

43 New England Genealogic Society

44 Charles River Associates

45 Boston Public

46 Boston Architecture

47 Massachusetts Historical Society

48 Christian Science Monitor

49 Massachusetts Horticultural Society

50 Franklin Institute

51 Boston Herald Newspaper

KEY

37 Public Libraries

38 Professional Libraries

Listed Alphabetically

PUBLIC

Adams St, 29. 690 Adams St, Dorchester ☎ 436-6900

Boston Public, 45. 666 Boylston St ☎ 536-5400

Brighton, 5. 40 Academy Hill Rd, Brighton ☎ 782-6032

Charlestown, 30. 179 Main St, Charlestown ☎ 242-1248

Codman Sq, 27. 690 Washington St, Dorchester ☎ 436-8214

Connolly, 14. 433 Centre St, Jamaica Plain ☎ 522-1960

Dudley, 11. 65 Warren St, Roxbury ☎ 442-6186

East Boston, 2. 276 Meridian St, E Boston ☎ 569-0271

Egleston Sq, 15. 2044 Columbus Ave, Roxbury ☎ 445-4340

Faneuil, 4. 419 Faneuil St, Brighton ☎ 782-6705

Fields Corner, 22. 1520 Dorchester Ave, Dorchester ☎ 436-2155

Grove Hall, 18. 5 Crawford St, Roxbury ☎ 427-3337

Hyde Park, 26. 35 Harvard St, Hyde Park ☎ 361-2524

Jamaica Plain, 17. 12 Sedgwick St, Jamaica Plain ☎ 524-2053

Kirstein Business, 36. 20 City Hall Ave ☎ 523-0860

Lower Mills, 28. 27 Richmond St, Dorchester ☎ 298-7841

Mattapan, 25. 10 Hazelton St, Mattapan ☎ 298-9218

North End, 31. 25 Parmenter St ☎ 227-8135

Orient Heights, 3. 18 Barnes Ave, E Boston ☎ 567-2516

Parker Hill, 10. 1497 Tremont St, Roxbury ☎ 427-3820

Roslindale, 24. 4238 Washington St, Roslindale ☎ 323-2343

South Boston, 13. 646 E Broadway, S Boston ☎ 268-0180

Uphams Corner, 19. 500 Columbia Rd, Dorchester ☎ 265-0139

Washington Village, 12. 1226 Columbia Rd, S Boston ☎ 269-7239

West End, 32. 151 Cambridge St ☎ 523-3957

West Roxbury, 23. 1961 Centre St, W Roxbury ☎ 325-3147

PROFESSIONAL

Archives of American Art, 33. 87 Mt Vernon St ☎ 565-8444

Arnold Arboretum, 16. Arborway, Jamaica Plain ☎ 524-1718

Art Institute Boston, 7. 700 Beacon St ☎ 262-1223

Boston Architecture, 46. 320 Newbury St ☎ 262-5000

Boston Athenaeum, 35. 10½ Beacon St ☎ 227-0270

Boston Globe Newspaper, 20. 135 Morrissey Blvd ☎ 929-2000

Boston Herald Newspaper, 51. One Herald Sq ☎ 426-3000

Boston Psychoanalytic, 40. 15 Commonwealth Ave ☎ 266-0953

Bostonian Society, 37. 15 State St ☎ 720-3285

Charles River Associates, 44. 200 Clarendon St ☎ 266-0500

Christian Science Monitor, 48. 1 Norway St ☎ 450-2000

Congregational Library, 34. 14 Beacon St ☎ 523-0470

Crime & Justice Foundation, 41. 95 Berkeley St ☎ 426-9800

Federal Reserve Bank, 42. 600 Atlantic Ave ☎ 973-3397

Franklin Institute, 50. 41 Berkeley St ☎ 423-4630

French Library, 39. 53 Marlborough St ☎ 266-4351

Goethe Institute, 38. 170 Beacon St ☎ 262-6050

Kennedy Presidential, 21. Columbia Pt, Dorchester ☎ 929-4500

Mass Historical Society, 47. 1154 Boylston St ☎ 536-1608

Mass Horticultural Society, 49. 300 Mass Ave ☎ 536-9280

Museum of Fine Arts, 9. 465 Huntington Ave ☎ 267-9300

New Eng Historic Genealogic Society, 43. 101 Newbury St ☎ 536-5740

Smithsonian Astrophysical, 1. 60 Garden St, Cambridge ☎ 495-7461

Temple Israel, 8. 260 Riverway ☎ 566-3960

Zion Research, 6. 771 Commonwealth Ave ☎ 353-3724

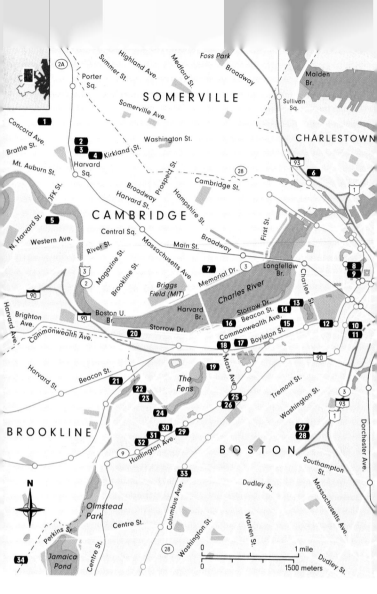

Listed by Site Number

1	Radcliffe College
2	Harvard Law
3	Lesley University
4	Harvard University
5	Harvard Business
6	Bunker Hill CC
7	Mass Inst Tech (MIT)
8	Suffolk University
9	Suffolk Law
10	Tufts Dental
11	Tufts Medical
12	New Eng Sch of Law
13	Fisher College
14	Emerson College
15	Bay State College
16	New Eng College of Optometry
17	Newbury College
18	Berklee Col of Music
19	Boston Conservatory of Music
20	Boston University
21	Hebrew College
22	Wheelock College
23	Emmanuel College
24	Simmons College
25	New England Conservatory of Music
26	Northeastern Univ
27	Boston Univ Dental
28	Boston Univ Medical
29	Wentworth Inst Tech
30	Mass College of Art
31	Mass Col Pharmacy
32	Harvard Medical
33	Roxbury CC
34	Hellenic College

Listed Alphabetically

Bay State College, 15.
122 Commonwealth Ave
☎ 236-8000

Berklee College of Music, 18.
1140 Boylston St
☎ 266-1400

Boston Conservatory of Music, 19.
8 Fenway
☎ 536-6340

Boston University, 20.
770 Commonwealth Ave
☎ 353-2000

Boston University Medical Center Campus, 28.
88 E Newton St
☎ 638-8000

Boston University Medical Center–Goldman Graduate School of Dentistry, 27. 100 E Newton St
☎ 638-4700

Bunker Hill Community College, 6.
Rutherford Ave, Charlestown
☎ 228-2000

Emerson College, 14.
100 Beacon St
☎ 824-8500

Emmanuel College, 23.
400 The Fenway
☎ 277-9340

Fisher College, 13.
118 Beacon St
☎ 236-8800

Harvard Business School, 5.
16 No Harvard St
☎ 495-6000

Harvard Law School, 2.
Massachusetts Ave, Cambridge
☎ 495-3100

Harvard Medical, 32.
25 Shattuck St
☎ 432-1000

Harvard University, 4.
33 Kirkland St, Cambridge
☎ 495-1000

Hebrew College, 21.
43 Hawes St, Brookline
☎ 232-8710

Hellenic College, 34.
50 Goddard Ave, Brookline
☎ 731-3500

Lesley University, 3.
29 Everett St, Cambridge
☎ 868-9600

Massachusetts College of Art, 30.
621 Huntington Ave
☎ 232-1555

Massachusetts College of Pharmacy and Allied Health Sciences, 31.
179 Longwood Ave
☎ 732-2800

Massachusetts Institute of Technology (MIT), 7.
77 Massachusetts Ave, Cambridge
☎ 253-1000

New England College of Optometry, 16.
424 Beacon St
☎ 266-2030

New England Conservatory of Music, 25.
290 Huntington Ave
☎ 585-1100

New England School of Law, 12.
154 Stuart St
☎ 451-0010

Newbury College, 17.
129 Fisher Ave, Brookline
☎ 730-7000

Northeastern University, 26.
360 Huntington Ave
☎ 373-2000

Radcliffe College, 1.
10 Garden St, Cambridge
☎ 495-8601

Roxbury Community College, 33.
1234 Columbus Ave, Roxbury
☎ 427-0060

Simmons College, 24.
300 The Fenway
☎ 521-2000

Suffolk University, 8.
8 Ashburton Pl
☎ 573-8000

Suffolk University Law School, 9.
41 Temple St
☎ 573-8000

Tufts University School of Dental Medicine, 10.
1 Kneeland St
☎ 636-6828

Tufts University School of Medicine, 11. 136 Harrison Ave
☎ 636-7000

Wentworth Institute of Technology, 29.
550 Huntington Ave
☎ 442-9010

Wheelock College, 22.
200 Riverway
☎ 734-5200

MAP **13** Universities & Colleges/Boston Area

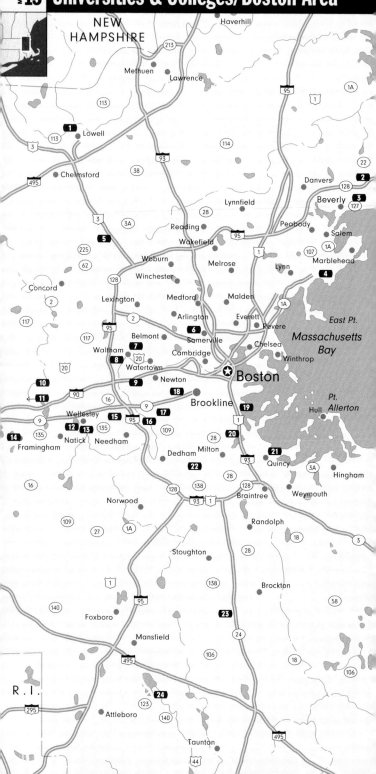

NEW
HAMPSHIRE

Haverhill

(213)

Methuen
Lawrence

(95)

(1A)

(113)

(1)

1 Lowell
(113)

(3)

(93)

(114)

(22)

Chelmsford

(495)

(38)

Danvers
(128)

2

Lynnfield

Beverly
3
(127)

(3)

(3A)

Reading
(28)

Peabody

Salem

Wakefield

(95)

(1A)

5

(225)

Woburn

Melrose

(1)

(107)

Marblehead

(62)

Winchester

Lynn

4

Concord

(128)

(2)

Lexington

Medford

Malden

East Pt.

(117)

(2)

Arlington

Everett

(1A)

Massachusetts

(95)

6

Revere

Bay

(117)

Belmont

Somerville

Chelsea

Waltham
7

Cambridge

Winthrop

8

(20)

10

Watertown

(20)

Boston

9

Newton

18

Pt.

11

(90)

Brookline

19

Allerton

(16)

Hull

(9)

(9)

17

(1)

Wellesley
15

20

14

(9)

12 **13** (135)

16

(28)

(135)

(95)

(109)

21

(16)

Natick

Needham

Dedham

Milton

Quincy

(3A)

Hingham

(28)

22

(128)

(138)

(128)

Braintree

Weymouth

Norwood

(93) (1)

(109)

(27)

(1A)

Randolph

(18)

(3)

Stoughton

(28)

(140)

(138)

Brockton

(58)

Foxboro

(95)

23

Mansfield

(24)

R.I.

(106)

(18)

(106)

(295)

24

(123)

(495)

Attleboro

(140)

Taunton

(44)

Listed by Site Number

1 University of Massachusetts–Lowell
2 Gordon College
3 Endicott College
4 Salem State College
5 Middlesex Community College
6 Tufts University
7 Bentley College
8 Brandeis University
9 Lasell College
10 Regis College
11 Tufts University School of Veterinary Medicine
12 Wellesley College
13 Babson College
14 Framingham State
15 Massachusetts Bay Community College
16 Mount Ida College
17 Pine Manor College
18 Boston College
19 University of Massachusetts–Boston
20 Laboure College
21 Eastern Nazarene College
22 Curry College
23 Stonehill College
24 Wheaton College

Listed Alphabetically

Babson College, 13.
Wellesley Ave, Wellesley
☎ 781/235-1200

Bentley College, 7.
175 Forest St, Waltham
☎ 781/891-2000

Boston College, 18.
140 Commonwealth Ave, Newton
☎ 552-8000

Brandeis University, 8.
415 South St, Waltham
☎ 781/736-2000

Curry College, 22.
1071 Blue Hill Ave, Milton
☎ 333-0500

Eastern Nazarene College, 21.
23 E Elm St, Quincy ☎ 745-3000

Endicott College, 3.
376 Hale St, Beverly
☎ 978/927-0585

Framinham State College, 14.
100 State St, Framingham
☎ 508/620-1220

Gordon College, 2.
255 Grapevine Rd, Wenham
☎ 978/927-2300

Laboure College, 20.
2120 Dorchester Ave
☎ 296-8300

Lasell College, 9.
1844 Commonwealth Ave, Newton
☎ 243-2000

Massachusetts Bay Community College, 15.
50 Oakland St, Wellesley
☎ 781/237-1100

Middlesex Community College, 5.
Springs Rd, Bedford
☎ 781/280-3200

Mount Ida College, 16.
777 Dedham St, Newton
☎ 969-7000

Pine Manor College, 17.
400 Heath St, Newton
☎ 731-7000

Regis College, 10.
235 Wellesley St, Weston
☎ 781/893-1820

Salem State College, 4.
352 Lafayette St, Salem
☎ 978/741-6000

Stonehill College, 23.
320 Washington Ave, Easton
☎ 508/565-1000

Tufts University, 6.
Packard Ave, Medford
☎ 628-5000

Tufts University School of Veterinary Medicine, 11.
Westboro Rd, North Grafton
☎ 508/839-5302

University of Massachusetts–Boston, 19.
Columbia Bay
☎ 287-5000

University of Massachusetts–Lowell, 1.
1 University Ave, Lowell
☎ 978/934-4000

Wellesley College, 12.
106 Central St, Wellesley
☎ 781/283-1000

Wheaton College, 24.
E Main St, Norton
☎ 508/285-7722

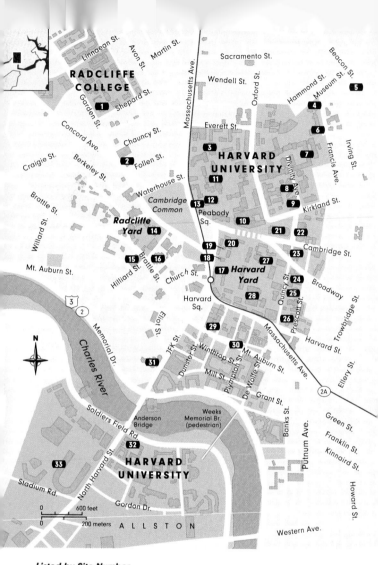

Listed by Site Number

1   Hilles Library
2   Longy Sch of Music
3   Harkness Commons & The Graduate Ctr
4   Rockefeller Hall
5   American Academy of Arts & Sciences
6   Divinity School
7   Harvard Biological Laboratories
8   Sherman Fairchild Biochemistry Lab
9   Adolphus Busch Hall
10   Science Center

11   Law School
12   Austin Hall
13   Hemenway Gym
14   Byerly Hall
15   Loeb Drama Center
16   Gutman Library
17   Massachusetts Hall
18   Harvard Hall
19   Holden Chapel
20   Stoughton Hall
21   Memorial Hall/ Sanders Theater
22   George Gund Hall
23   Arthur M Sackler

Museum
24   Fogg Museum
25   Carpenter Center for the Visual Arts
26   Harvard Union
27   Memorial Church
28   Widener Library
29   Holyoke Center
30   Harvard Lampoon Castle
31   Kennedy Sch of Gov't
32   Harvard Business School
33   Soldiers Field

Massachusetts Institute of Technology M15

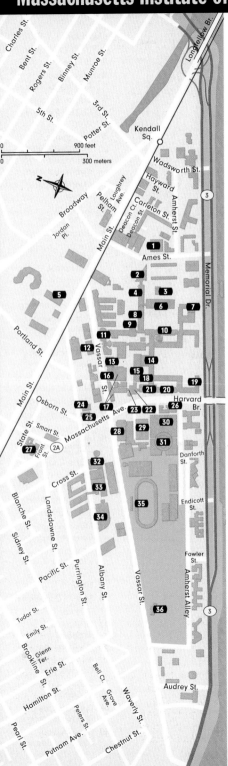

Listed by Site Number

1 List Visual Arts Centre
2 Ralph Landau Building
3 Green Building
4 Whitaker Building
5 Laboratory for Computer Science
6 Dreyfus Building
7 Hayden Memorial Library
8 Dorrance Building
9 Compton Labs
10 Eastman Labs
11 Fairchild Building
12 Cyclotron
13 Brown Building
14 Maclaurin Bldgs
15 Bush Building
16 McNair Building
17 Sloan Laboratories
18 Homberg Building
19 Pierce Laboratory
20 Pratt School
21 Rogers Bldg/Hart Nautical Gallery
22 Center for Advanced Engineering Study
23 Guggenheim Lab
24 Superconducting Generator Test Facility
25 High Voltage Research Lab
26 Center for Advanced Visual Studies
27 MIT Museum
28 du Pont Athletic Center
29 Stratton Building Student Center
30 MIT Chapel
31 Kresge Auditorium
32 Nuclear Reactor Laboratory
33 F Bitter National Magnet Laboratory
34 Nabisco Lab
35 Steinbrenner Stadium
36 MIT Solar Demo Building

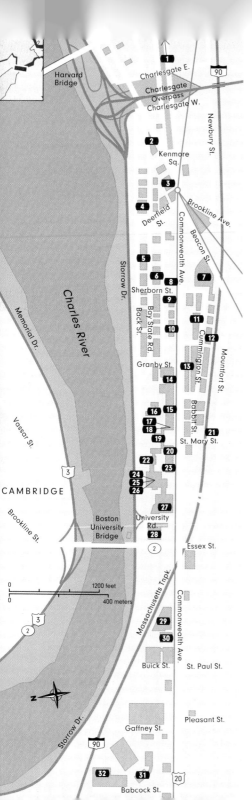

Listed by Site Number

1   BU Theatre
2   Myles Standish Residential Area
3   Barnes & Noble
4   Shelton Residential Area
5   Admissions Reception Center
6   The Towers Residential Area
7   Metcalf Science Center
8   School of Management
9   School of Education
10 Sargent College of Allied Health Professions
11 College of Communication
12 Col of Engineering
13 Warren Towers Residential Complex
14 Tsai Performance Center
15 Graduate School of Arts & Sciences
16 Sch of Social Work
17 College of Liberal Arts
18 Judson Boardman Coit Observatory
19 Marsh Chapel
20 School of Theology
21 South Campus Residential Area
22 School of Law
23 Metropolitan College
24 University Information Center
25 Mugar Memorial Library
26 Special Collections
27 Sherman Union
28 Boston Univ Academy
29 School for the Arts/ Art Gallery/ Concert Hall
30 College of General Studies
31 West Campus Residential Area
32 Case Physical Education Center

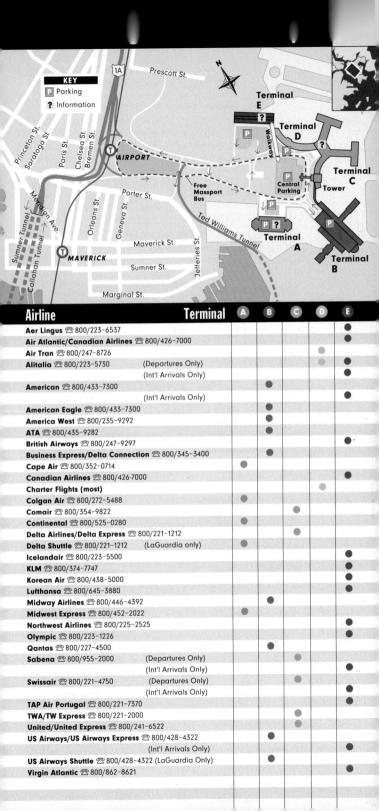

Airline	Terminal	A	B	C	D	E
Aer Lingus ☎ 800/223-6537						●
Air Atlantic/Canadian Airlines ☎ 800/426-7000						●
Air Tran ☎ 800/247-8726					●	
Alitalia ☎ 800/223-5730 (Departures Only)					●	
(Int'l Arrivals Only)						●
American ☎ 800/433-7300			●			
(Int'l Arrivals Only)						●
American Eagle ☎ 800/433-7300			●			
America West ☎ 800/235-9292			●			
ATA ☎ 800/435-9282			●			
British Airways ☎ 800/247-9297						●
Business Express/Delta Connection ☎ 800/345-3400			●			
Cape Air ☎ 800/352-0714		●				
Canadian Airlines ☎ 800/426-7000						●
Charter Flights (most)					●	
Colgan Air ☎ 800/272-5488		●				
Comair ☎ 800/354-9822				●		
Continental ☎ 800/525-0280		●				
Delta Airlines/Delta Express ☎ 800/221-1212				●		
Delta Shuttle ☎ 800/221-1212 (LaGuardia only)		●				
Icelandair ☎ 800/223-5500						●
KLM ☎ 800/374-7747						●
Korean Air ☎ 800/438-5000						●
Lufthansa ☎ 800/645-3880						●
Midway Airlines ☎ 800/446-4392			●			
Midwest Express ☎ 800/452-2022		●				
Northwest Airlines ☎ 800/225-2525						●
Olympic ☎ 800/223-1226						●
Qantas ☎ 800/227-4500			●			
Sabena ☎ 800/955-2000 (Departures Only)				●		
(Int'l Arrivals Only)						●
Swissair ☎ 800/221-4750 (Departures Only)				●		
(Int'l Arrivals Only)						●
TAP Air Portugal ☎ 800/221-7370						●
TWA/TW Express ☎ 800/221-2000				●		
United/United Express ☎ 800/241-6522				●		
US Airways/US Airways Express ☎ 800/428-4322			●			
(Int'l Arrivals Only)						●
US Airways Shuttle ☎ 800/428-4322 (LaGuardia Only)			●			
Virgin Atlantic ☎ 800/862-8621						●

KEY
P Parking
? Information

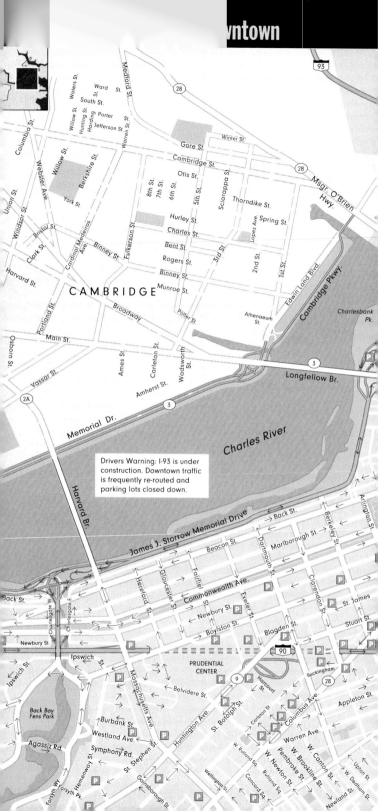

93

Waters St.
Ward St.
South St.
Willow St.
Hunting St.
Harding St.
Porter St.
Jefferson St.
Warren St.
Medford St.
Columbia St.
Webster Ave.
Willow St.
Berkshire St.
York St.
Union St.
Windsor St.
Bristol St.
Clark St.
Harvard St.
Cardinal Medeiros Ave.
Binney St.
Fulkerson St.
Portland St.
Main St.
Osborn St.
Vassar St.

28

Gore St.
Winter St.
Cambridge St.
Otis St.
8th St.
7th St.
6th St.
5th St.
Sciarappa St.
Thorndike St.
Spring St.
Hurley St.
Charles St.
Bent St.
Rogers St.
Binney St.
Munroe St.
Lopez Ave.
3rd St.
2nd St.
1st St.

28

Msgr. O'Brien Hwy.

Edwin Land Blvd.
Cambridge Pkwy.
Charlesbank Pk.

CAMBRIDGE

Broadway
Ames St.
Carleton St.
Wadsworth St.
Amherst St.
Potter St.
Athenaeum St.

3

Longfellow Br.

2A

Memorial Dr.

Harvard Br.

Charles River

3

Drivers Warning: I-93 is under construction. Downtown traffic is frequently re-routed and parking lots closed down.

James J. Storrow Memorial Drive

Back St.
Back St.
Charlesgate W.
Charlesgate E.
Beacon St.
Marlborough St.
Berkeley St.
Arlington St.
Newbury St.
Hereford St.
Gloucester St.
Fairfield St.
Dartmouth St.
Clarendon St.
St. James
Commonwealth Ave.
Exeter St.
Newbury St.
Boylston St.
Blagden St.
Stuart St.
Ipswich St.
Ipswich St.

90

Buckingham
PRUDENTIAL CENTER

9

Belvidere St.
Harcourt St.
Columbus Ave.
Appleton St.

28

Massachusetts Ave.
St. Botolph St.
Carleton St.
Burbank St.
Westland Ave.
Huntington Ave.
Warren Ave.
W. Canton St.
Columbus Ave.
Symphony Rd.
St. Stephen St.
W. Rutland Sq.
W. Newton St.
W. Brookline St.
W. Dedham St.
Upton St.
Back Bay Fens Park
Agassiz Rd.
Gainsborough St.
Wellington St.
Rutland Sq.
Pembroke St.
Concord Sq.
Newland St.
Forsyth Wy.
Forsyth St.
Forsyth Pk.
Hemenway St.

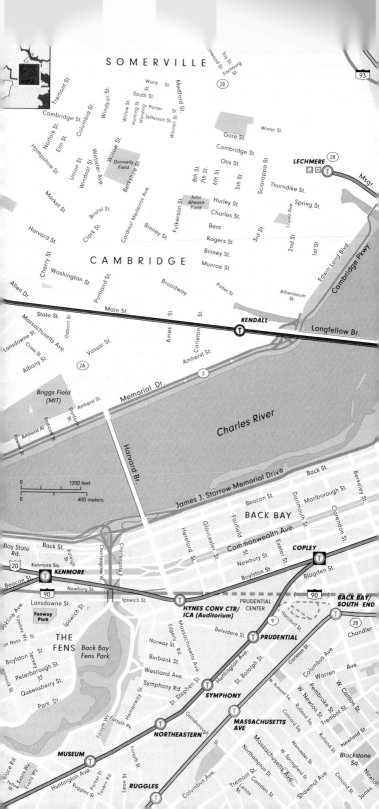

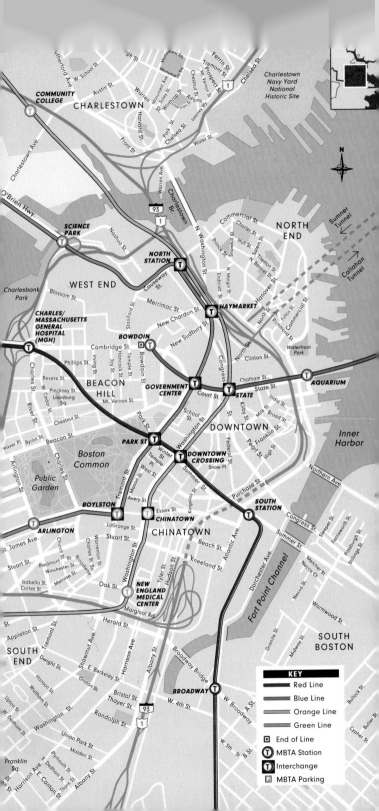

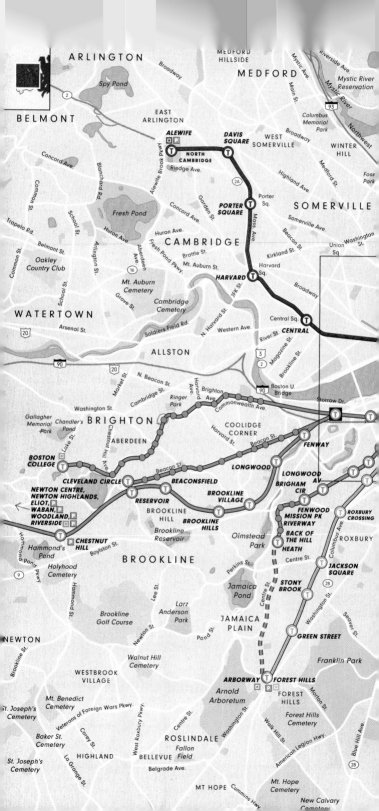

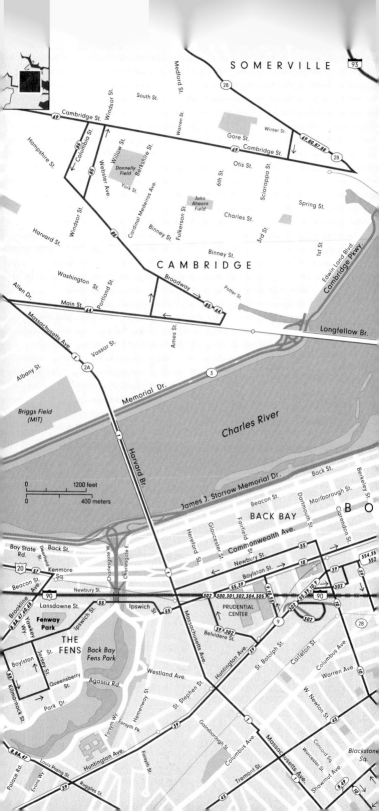

MAP 23 Commuter Rail Lines & Outer Ⓣ Stops

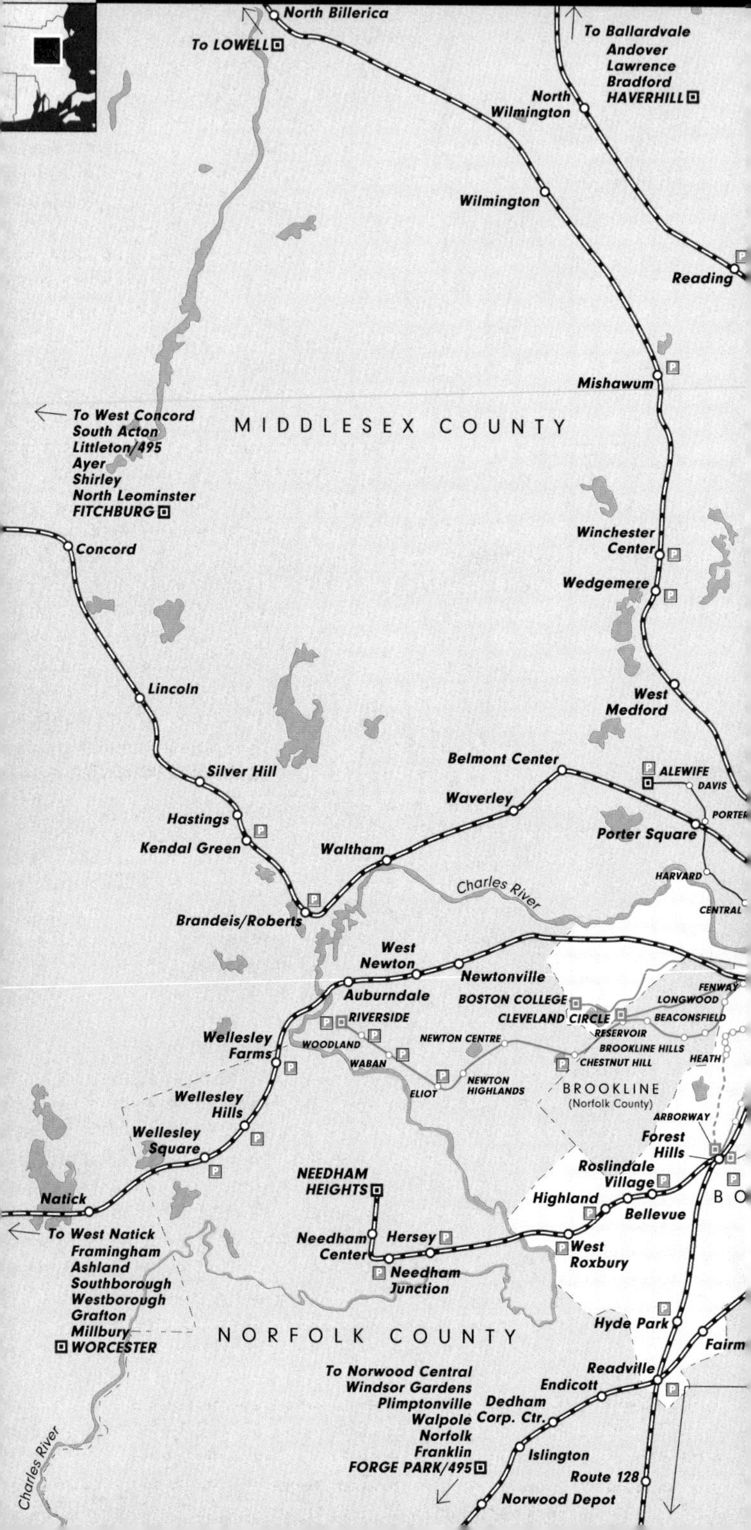
North Billerica
To LOWELL
To Ballardvale
Andover
Lawrence
Bradford
HAVERHILL
North Wilmington
Wilmington
Reading
Mishawum
To West Concord
South Acton
Littleton/495
Ayer
Shirley
North Leominster
FITCHBURG
MIDDLESEX COUNTY
Concord
Winchester Center
Wedgemere
Lincoln
West Medford
Silver Hill
Belmont Center
ALEWIFE
DAVIS
Hastings
Waverley
PORTER
Kendal Green
Waltham
Porter Square
HARVARD
Charles River
CENTRAL
Brandeis/Roberts
West Newton
Newtonville
Auburndale
BOSTON COLLEGE
FENWAY
LONGWOOD
CLEVELAND CIRCLE
BEACONSFIELD
RIVERSIDE
RESERVOIR
Wellesley Farms
WOODLAND
NEWTON CENTRE
BROOKLINE HILLS
WABAN
CHESTNUT HILL
HEATH
NEWTON HIGHLANDS
ELIOT
BROOKLINE
(Norfolk County)
Wellesley Hills
ARBORWAY
Wellesley Square
Forest Hills
Roslindale Village
NEEDHAM HEIGHTS
Natick
Highland
Bellevue
BO
To West Natick
Framingham
Ashland
Southborough
Westborough
Grafton
Millbury
WORCESTER
Needham Center
Hersey
West Roxbury
Needham Junction
NORFOLK COUNTY
Hyde Park
Fairm
Readville
To Norwood Central
Windsor Gardens
Plimptonville
Walpole
Norfolk
Franklin
FORGE PARK/495
Endicott
Dedham Corp. Ctr.
Islington
Route 128
Norwood Depot
Charles River

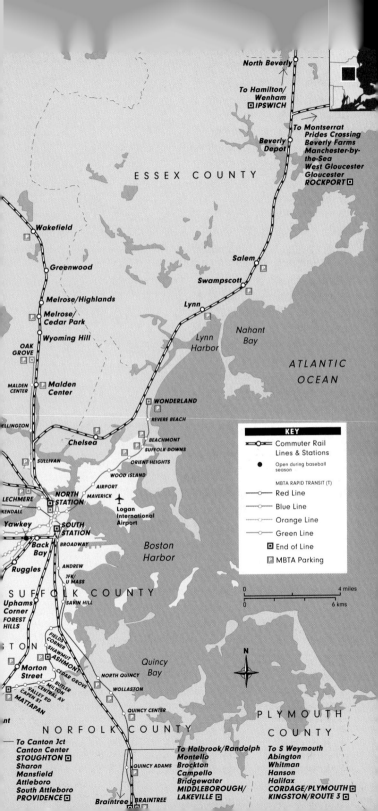

North Beverly

To Hamilton/
Wenham
IPSWICH

To Montserrat
Prides Crossing
Beverly Farms
Manchester-by-
the-Sea
West Gloucester
Gloucester
ROCKPORT

Beverly
Depot

ESSEX COUNTY

Wakefield

Greenwood

Salem

Swampscott

Melrose/Highlands

Lynn

Melrose/
Cedar Park

Wyoming Hill

OAK
GROVE

MALDEN
CENTER

Malden
Center

Nahant
Bay

Lynn
Harbor

ATLANTIC
OCEAN

ELLINGTON

WONDERLAND

Chelsea

REVERE BEACH

BEACHMONT

SUFFOLK DOWNS

SULLIVAN

ORIENT HEIGHTS

WOOD ISLAND

NORTH
STATION

AIRPORT

LECHMERE

MAVERICK

KENDALL

SOUTH
STATION

Logan
International
Airport

Yawkey

BROADWAY

Back
Bay

Boston
Harbor

ANDREW

Ruggles

JFK/
U MASS

SUFFOLK   COUNTY

SAVIN HILL

Uphams
Corner
FOREST
HILLS

FIELDS
CORNER

STON

SHAWMUT
ASHMONT

Quincy
Bay

Morton
Street

CEDAR GROVE

NORTH QUINCY

BUTLER

MILTON

WOLLASTON

VALLEY RD

CENTRAL AV

CAPEN ST

MATTAPAN

QUINCY CENTER

PLYMOUTH

NORFOLK   COUNTY

COUNTY

To Canton Jct
Canton Center
STOUGHTON
Sharon
Mansfield
Attleboro
South Attleboro
PROVIDENCE

QUINCY ADAMS

To Holbrook/Randolph
Montello
Brockton
Campello
Bridgewater
MIDDLEBOROUGH/
LAKEVILLE

To S Weymouth
Abington
Whitman
Hanson
Halifax
CORDAGE/PLYMOUTH
KINGSTON/ROUTE 3

Braintree   BRAINTREE

nt

N

0   4 miles
0   6 kms

KEY	
Commuter Rail Lines & Stations	
Open during baseball season	

MBTA RAPID TRANSIT (T)
Red Line
Blue Line
Orange Line
Green Line
End of Line
MBTA Parking

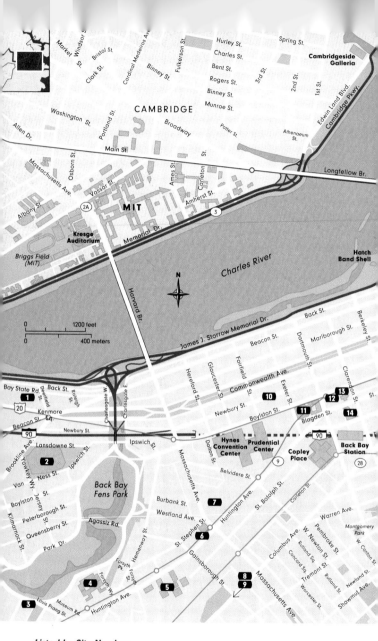

Listed by Site Number

1	Boston University	7	Christian Science Headquarters	14	John Hancock Tower Observatory
2	Fenway Park	8	Franklin Park Zoo	15	Arlington St Church
3	Isabella Stewart Gardner Museum	9	Arnold Arboretum	16	Public Garden (Swan Boats)
4	Museum of Fine Arts	10	Newbury Street	17	Bull & Finch Pub (Cheers)
5	Northeastern University	11	Boston Public Library	18	Wang Center
6	Symphony Hall	12	Copley Square		
		13	Trinity Church		

Listed by Site Number (cont.)

19 Chinatown
20 Boston Tea Party Ship & Museum
21 St Paul's Cathedral
22 Park Street Church
23 State House
24 African Meeting House
25 King's Chapel & Cemetery
26 Old City Hall
27 Old State House
28 Faneuil Hall
29 Union Oyster House
30 Quincy Market
31 Custom House & Tower
32 New England Aquarium
33 Old North Church
34 FleetCenter
35 USS Constitution
36 Museum of Science

MAP **25** Freedom Trail & Black Heritage Trail

99

Main St.
School St.
Elm St.
High St.
Cross St.
Cedar St.
Green St.
Monument Sq.
Lexington St.
Ferrin St.
Tremont St.
Mt. Vernon St.
Decatur St.
Chelsea St.

1

Rutherford Ave.
Austin St.
Cordis St.
Warren St.
Pleasant St.
Monument Ave.
Chestnut St.
Mt. Vernon St.
Adams St.
Lowney Wy.

Union St.
Washington St.
Lynde St.
Main St.
Harvard St.
Huron St.
Soley St.
Winthrop St.
Park St.
Chelsea St.

16

Charlestown Navy Yard National Historic Site

CHARLESTOWN

Charlestown Ave.
Front St.
Wapping St.
Water St.

15 **USS Constitution**

CAMBRIDGE

Msgr. O'Brien Hwy.

Museum of Science

Hayden Planetarium

Nashua St.

Charlestown Br.
N. Washington St.

93

1

Commercial St.
Charter St.
Hull St.
Snowhill St.
Prince St.
Salem St.
N. Margin St.
N. Bennet St.
Hanover Ave.
Harris St.
Clark St.

14

13

Lomasney Wy.
Causeway St.
Haverhill St.
Friend St.
Canal St.
Merrimac St.
Endicott St.

North Station/ FleetCenter

Charlesbank Park

Charles St.
Fruit St.
Blossom St.
N. Grove St.
Parkman St.

New Chardon St.

New Sudbury St.

Hanover St.
Fleet St.
Hanover St.

12

North St.
Cross St.
Commercial St.

Cambridge St.

Phillips St.
7
Revere St.
BEACON HILL
6 **4**
Smith Ct.
5
3

9
10
2

8
Cedar St.
W. Cedar St.
Charles St.
Grove St.
Garden St.
Mt. Vernon St.
River St.
Brimmer Pl.
Byron St.
Branch St.

Temple St.
Bowdoin St.
Hancock St.
Somerset St.
Pinckney St.
Vernon St.
Chestnut St.
Walnut St.

City Hall

Congress St.
Sudbury St.
Hanover St.
Union St.

11 **Quincy Market**
Chatham St.

2 **State House**

1

3

Park St.
Beacon St.

Court St.
School St.
5 **6**
7
8
Province St.
Bromfield St.
Washington St.
Winter St.
Temple Pl.
West St.
Mason St.
Devonshire St.
Arch St.
Summer St.
Federal St.
Otis St.
Snow Pl.

10
9

State St.
India St.
Kilby St.
Milk St.
Broad St.
Oliver St.
Pearl St.
Franklin St.
High St.

Boston Common

1

Public Garden

Charles St.
Arlington St.

Tremont St.

Purchase Ave.
Atlantic Ave.

Congress St.

Essex St.

LaGrange St.

Eliot St.
Stuart St.
Church St.
Broadway
Charles St. S.
Tremont St.
Washington St.
Oak St.
Beach St.
Kneeland St.
Tyler St.
Hudson St.

South Station

Atlantic Ave.
Summer St.

Providence St.
James Ave.

Stuart St.

Isabella St.
Cortes St.
Berkeley St.

90

Chandler St.
Appleton St.
Tremont St.
E. Berkeley St.
Herald St.
Shawmut Ave.
Harrison Ave.
Marginal Rd.
Albany St.
Broadway Br.

93

1

Listed by Site Number

Freedom Trail

1 Boston Common
2 State House
3 Park St Church
4 Granary Burying Ground
5 King's Chapel
6 First Public School
7 Old Corner Bookstore
8 Old South Meeting House
9 Old State House
10 Boston Massacre Site
11 Faneuil Hall/Quincy Market
12 Paul Revere House
13 Old North Church
14 Copp's Hill Burying Ground
15 USS *Constitution*
16 Bunker Hill Monument

Black Heritage Trail

1 Robert Gould Shaw Memorial
2 George Middleton House
3 Abiel Smith School
4 African Meeting House
5 Smith Court Residences
6 Coburn's Gaming House
7 Lewis & Harriet Hayden House
8 Charles St Meeting House
9 John J Smith House
10 Phillips School

Listed Alphabetically

FREEDOM TRAIL (☎ 242-5642)

Boston Massacre Site, 10.
State & Devonshire Sts

Boston Common, 1. Park St

Bunker Hill Monument, 16.
Monument Sq, Charlestown

Copp's Hill Burying Ground, 14.
Charter St

Faneuil Hall, 11.
Faneuil Hall

First Public School, 6. School St

Granary Burying Ground, 4.
Tremont & Park Sts

King's Chapel, 5. 58 Tremont St

Old Corner Bookstore, 7.
3 School St

Old North Church, 13.
193 Salem St

Old South Meeting House, 8.
310 Washington St

Old State House, 9.
206 Washington St

Park St Church, 3. I Park St

Paul Revere House, 12. 19 North Sq

State House, 2. One Ashburton Pl

USS *Constitution*, 15.
Constitution Wharf, Charlestown

BLACK HERITAGE TRAIL (☎ 742-5415)

Abiel Smith School, 3.
46 Joy St

African Meeting House, 4.
8 Smith Court

Charles St Meeting House, 8.
Mt Vernon & Charles Sts

Coburn's Gaming House, 6.
2 Phillips St

George Middleton House, 2.
5–7 Pinckney St

John J Smith House, 9.
86 Pinckney St

Lewis & Harriet Hayden House, 7.
66 Phillips St

Phillips School, 10.
Anderson & Pinckney Sts

Robert Gould Shaw Memorial, 1.
Beacon & Park Sts

Smith Court Residences, 5.
2–6 Smith Court

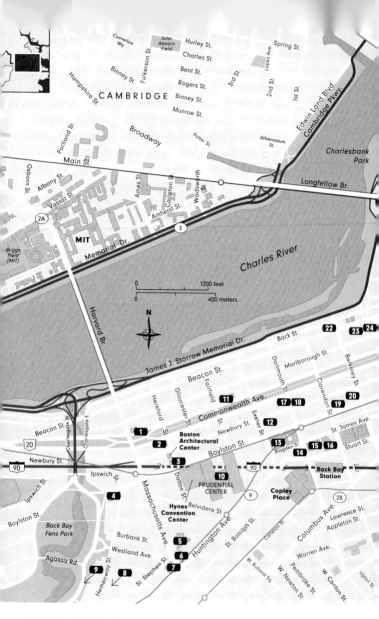

Listed by Site Number

1	Ames Mansion	**10**	Prudential Center	**20**	Louis Boston
2	Burrage Mansion	**11**	Algonquin Club	**21**	Cyclorama
3	Institute of Contemporary Art	**12**	Exeter St Theatre	**22**	Emerson College
4	Mass Historical Soc	**13**	Boston Public Library	**23**	Gibson House
5	Christian Science Ctr	**14**	Copley Place	**24**	Fisher Junior College
6	Horticultural Hall	**15**	Copley Plaza Hotel	**25**	Baylies Mansion
7	Symphony Hall	**16**	Hancock Tower	**26**	Colonial Theatre
8	Museum of Fine Arts	**17**	Hotel Vendome	**27**	Kennedy Library
9	Gardner Museum	**18**	270 Dartmouth St	**28**	Dorchester Heights Memorial
		19	The New England		

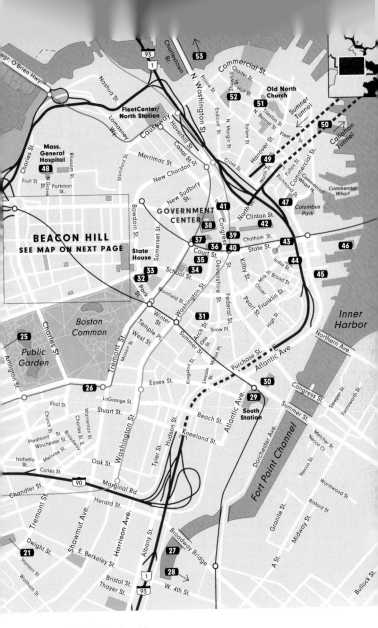

Listed by Site Number (cont.)

29 South Station
30 Federal Reserve Bank
31 89–93 Franklin St
32 Harding House
33 Boston Athenaeum
34 Old City Hall
35 Old Statehouse
36 Fleet Bank
37 Sears Crescent

38 City Hall
39 Faneuil Hall
40 60 State St
41 Blackstone Block
42 Quincy Market
43 Custom House
44 Flour & Grain
   Exchange
45 Harbor Towers

46 New England
   Aquarium
47 Mercantile Wharf
48 Mass General Hosp
49 Pierce-Hichborn Hse
50 Union Wharf
51 Clough House
52 44 Hull St
53 Bunker Hill
   Monument

Listed by Site Number

54 Charles St

55 Harrison Gray Otis House #1

56 43 S Russell St

57 Middleton-Glapion House

58 Massachusetts State House

59 17 Chestnut St

60 29A Chestnut St

61 Harrison Gray Otis House #2

62 Louisburg Square

63 Acorn St

64 Chestnut St

65 70–75 Beacon St

66 Harrison Gray Otis House #3

67 Somerset Club

68 Appleton-Parker Houses

69 34 Beacon St

Listed Alphabetically

Acorn St, 63.

Algonquin Club, 11.
217 Commonwealth Ave

Ames Mansion, 1.
355 Commonwealth Ave

Appleton-Parker Houses, 68.
39–40 Beacon St

Baylies Mansion, 25.
5 Commonwealth Ave

Blackstone Block, 41. Haymarket Sq

Boston Athenaeum, 33.
10½ Beacon St

Boston Public Library, 13.
666 Boylston St

Bunker Hill Monument, 53.
Monument Square

Burrage Mansion, 2.
314 Commonwealth Ave

Charles St, 54.

Chestnut St, 64.

Christian Science Center, 5.
175 Huntington Ave

City Hall, 38. I City Hall Square

Clough House, 51. 21 Unity St

Colonial Theatre, 26. 106 Boylston St

Copley Place, 14. I Copley Place

Copley Plaza Hotel, 15. Copley Sq

Custom House, 43. State & India Sts

Cyclorama, 21. 539 Tremont St

Dorchester Heights Memorial, 28.
Thomas Park/6th St, South Boston

89–93 Franklin St, 31.

Emerson College, 22. 100 Beacon St

Exeter St Theatre, 12. 26 Exeter St

Faneuil Hall, 39. Faneuil Hall
Marketplace

Federal Reserve Bank, 30.
600 Atlantic Ave

Fisher Junior College, 24. 118 Beacon St

Fleet Bank, 36. 28 State St

Flour & Grain Exchange, 44. 177 Milk St

43 S Russell St, 56.

44 Hull St, 52.

Gibson House, 23. 137 Beacon St

Hancock Tower, 16. Copley Square

Harbor Towers, 45. 85 E India Row

Harding House, 32. 16 Beacon St

**Harrison Gray Otis
House #1, 55.** 141 Cambridge St

**Harrison Gray Otis
House #2, 61.** 85 Mt Vernon St

**Harrison Gray Otis House #3,
66.** 45 Beacon St

Horticultural Hall, 6. 300 Mass Ave

Hotel Vendome, 17.
160 Commonwealth Ave

Institute of Contemporary Art, 3.
955 Boylston St

**Isabella Stewart Gardner
Museum, 9.** 280 Fenway

Kennedy Library, 27.
Columbia Pt, Dorchester

Louis Boston, 20. 234 Berkeley St

Louisburg Square, 62. Mt Vernon St

Mass General Hospital, 48. 55 Fruit St

Mass Historical Society, 4.
1154 Boylston St

Mass State House, 58. Beacon St

Mercantile Wharf, 47.
Atlantic Ave & Richmond St

Middleton-Glapion House, 57.
5 Pinckney St

Museum of Fine Arts, 8.
465 Huntington Ave

New England Aquarium, 46.
250 Atlantic Ave

Old City Hall, 34. 45 School St

Old Statehouse, 35. 206 Washington St

Pierce-Hichborn House, 49.
29 North Square

Prudential Center, 10. 800 Boylston St

Quincy Market, 42. Faneuil Hall
Marketplace

Sears Crescent, 37.
Government Center

17 Chestnut St, 59.

70–75 Beacon St, 65.

60 State St, 40.

Somerset Club, 67. 42 Beacon St

South Station, 29.
Summer St & Atlantic Ave

Symphony Hall, 7. 301 Mass Ave

The New England, 19. 501 Boylston St

34 Beacon St, 69.

29A Chestnut St, 60.

270 Dartmouth St, 18.

Union Wharf, 50. 323 Commercial St

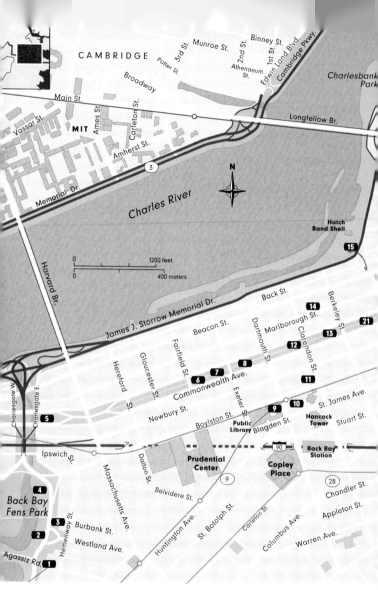

Listed by Site Number

1 Appeal to Great Spirit
2 Temple Bell
3 Memorial Fountain
4 John Boyle O'Reilly
5 Leif Erikson
6 Domingo Sarmiento
7 Adm Samuel Eliot Morison
8 Alexander Hamilton
9 Art & Science
9 Two Lions

10 Copley Square Fountain/Boston Marathon 100 Anniv
11 Phillips Brooks
12 Patrick Collins
13 John Glover
14 John Winthrop
15 Fiedler Footbridge
16 Geo White Memorial
17 Ducklings
18 Edward Everett Hale
19 Ether Memorial

20 George Washington
21 William Garrison
22 Boy & Bird Fountain
22 Small Child Fountain
22 Triton Babies Fountain
23 Kosciuszko Statue
24 Wendell Phillips
25 William E Channing
26 George Sumner
27 Col Thomas Cass
28 Boylston Place Gate

Listed by Site Number (cont.)

29 Boston Massacre	**40** Daniel Webster	**49** Hungarian Revolution
30 Soldiers & Sailors	**41** Cardinal Cushing	**50** Red Auerbach
31 Founders' Memorial	**42** Mary Dyer	**51** Samuel Adams
32 Aristides	**43** Rufus Choate	**52** Eagle (1798)
33 Columbus	**44** Joseph Tapping's Grave	**52** Grasshopper
34 Football Tablet	**45** Benjamin Franklin	**53** James Curley Memorial
35 Brewer Fountain	**46** Benjamin Franklin Bust	**54** Asarotan 1976
36 Col Robert Shaw	**47** Boston Bricks	**55** Mosaic Tiles
37 Henry Cabot Lodge	**48** New Post Office Square Fountain	**56** Fourteen Tablets
38 Anne Hutchinson		**56** Paul Revere
39 Nathaniel Banks		

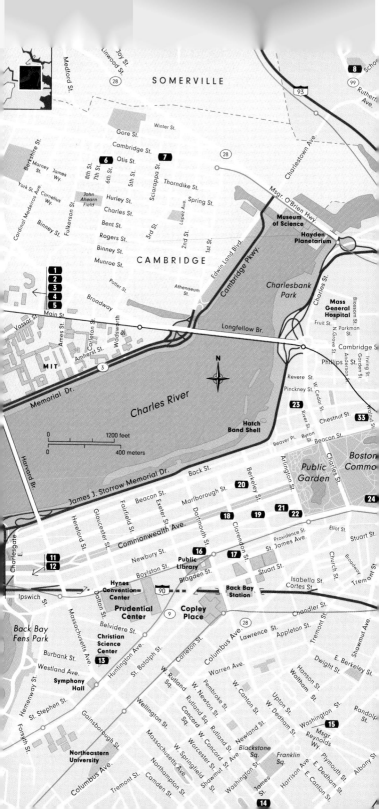

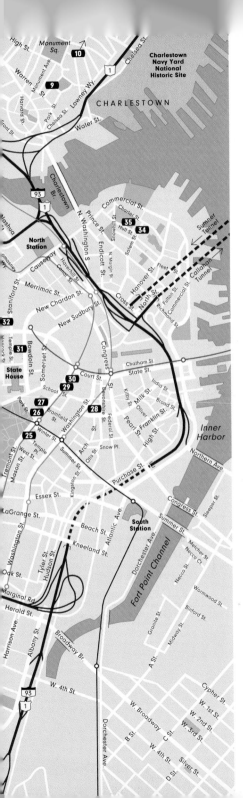

Listed by Site Number

1 Christ Church
2 First Parish Church
3 First Church Congregational
4 Mt Auburn Cemetery
5 Old Burying Ground
6 Sacred Heart Church
7 St Francis of Assisi
8 Phipps St Burying Ground
9 St Mary's
10 St Francis de Sales
11 Walter St Burying Ground
12 Temple Israel
13 Christian Science Mother Church
14 Church of the Immaculate Conception
15 Cathedral of the Holy Cross
16 Old South Church
17 Trinity Church
18 First Baptist Church of Boston
19 Church of the Covenant
20 First and Second Church of Boston
21 Emmanuel Episcopal
22 Arlington St Church
23 Church of the Advent
24 Central Burying Ground
25 St Paul's Cathedral
26 Park St Church
27 Granary Burying Ground
28 Old South Meeting House
29 King's Chapel
30 King's Chapel Burying Ground
31 St John Evangelist
32 Old West Church
33 Society of Friends
34 Christ Church (Old North)
35 Copp's Hill Burying Ground

Listed Alphabetically

CHURCHES

Arlington St Church, 22.
351 Boylston St ☎ 536-7050.
Unitarian-Universalist.

Cathedral of the Holy Cross, 15.
1400 Washington St
☎ 542-5682. Catholic.

Christ Church, 1. Zero Garden St,
Cambridge ☎ 876-0200. Episcopal.

Christ Church (Old North), 34.
193 Salem St ☎ 523-6676. Episcopal.

**Christian Science Mother
Church, 13.** 175 Huntington Ave
☎ 450-2000.

Church of the Advent, 23.
30 Brimmer St ☎ 523-2377.
Episcopal.

Church of the Covenant, 19.
67 Newbury St ☎ 266-7480.
Presbyterian.

**Church of the Immaculate
Conception, 14.** 775 Harrison St
☎ 536-8440. Catholic.

Emmanuel Episcopal, 21.
15 Newbury St ☎ 536-3355.

First Baptist Church of Boston, 18.
110 Commonwealth Ave ☎ 267-3148.

**First and Second Church of
Boston, 20.** 66 Marlborough St
☎ 267-6730. Unitarian-Universalist.

First Church Congregational, 3.
11 Garden St, Cambridge ☎ 547-2724.

First Parish Church, 2. 3 Church St,
Cambridge ☎ 876-7772.
Unitarian-Universalist.

King's Chapel, 29. 58 Tremont St
☎ 523-1749. Unitarian-Universalist.

Old South Church, 16.
645 Boylston St ☎ 536-1970.
United Church of Christ.

Old South Meeting House, 28.
294 Washington St ☎ 482-6439

Old West Church, 32.
131 Cambridge St
☎ 227-5088. Methodist.

Park St Church, 26. 1 Park St
☎ 523-3383. Congregational.

Sacred Heart Church, 6. 49 Sixth St,
Cambridge ☎ 547-0399. Catholic.

St Francis de Sales, 10.
303 Bunker Hill, Charlestown
☎ 242-0147. Catholic.

St Francis of Assisi, 7.
42 Sciarappa St, Cambridge
☎ 876-6754. Catholic.

St John Evangelist, 31.
35 Bowdoin St ☎ 227-5242.
Episcopal.

St Mary's, 9. 46 Winthrop St,
Charlestown ☎ 242-2196. Catholic.

St Paul's Cathedral, 25.
138 Tremont St ☎ 482-5800.
Episcopal.

Society of Friends, 33. 6 Chestnut St
☎ 227-9118. Quaker.

Temple Israel, 12. 260 Riverway
☎ 566-3960. Jewish.

Trinity Church, 17. Copley Square
☎ 536-0944. Episcopal.

CEMETERIES

Central Burying Ground, 24.
Tremont St/Boston Common

Copp's Hill Burying Ground, 35.
Charter St

Granary Burying Ground, 27. Park &
Tremont Sts

King's Chapel Burying Ground, 30.
58 Tremont St

Mt Auburn Cemetery, 4.
Mt Auburn St, Cambridge

**Old Burying Ground (First Parish
Church), 5.** Garden St, Cambridge

Phipps St Burying Ground, 8.
Phipps St, Charlestown

Walter St Burying Ground, 11.
Arnold Arboretum, Roslindale

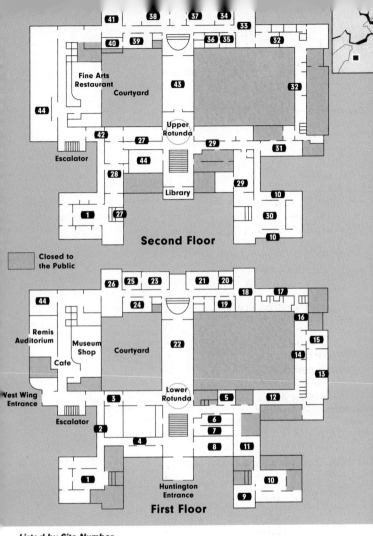

Second Floor

Fine Arts Restaurant
Courtyard
Escalator
Library
Upper Rotunda

Closed to the Public

First Floor

Remis Auditorium
Museum Shop
Cafe
Courtyard
West Wing Entrance
Escalator
Lower Rotunda
Huntington Entrance

Listed by Site Number

1 Japanese Art
2 Islamic Art
3 Brown Gallery
4 Indian Art
5 Egyptian Mummies
6 Graphics
7 Musical Instruments
8 Nubian Art
9 Etruscan Art
10 Greek Art
11 Near-Eastern Art
12 18th-C Amer Furniture
13 18th-C French Art
14 18th-C Boston
15 English Silver

16 19th-C American
17 American Federal
18 Copley
19 American Neo-Classic & Romantic
20 Amer Folk Painting
21 19th-C Landscape
22 American Modern
23 American Masters
24 Early 20th-C Amer
25 Amer Impressionism
26 20th-C Amer & Euro
27 Chinese Art
28 Bernat Galleries
29 Egyptian Art

30 Roman Art
31 Medieval Art
32 Euro Decorative Arts
33 Impressionism
34 19th-C French & Eng
35 Post-Impressionism
36 Coolidge Collection
37 18th-C Italian
38 Dutch & Flemish Art
39 Renaissance
40 Spanish Chapel
41 Baroque Art
42 Himalayan Art
43 Tapestries
44 Special Exhibitions

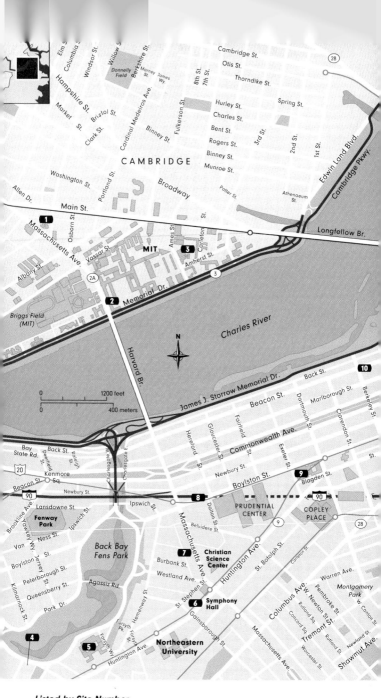

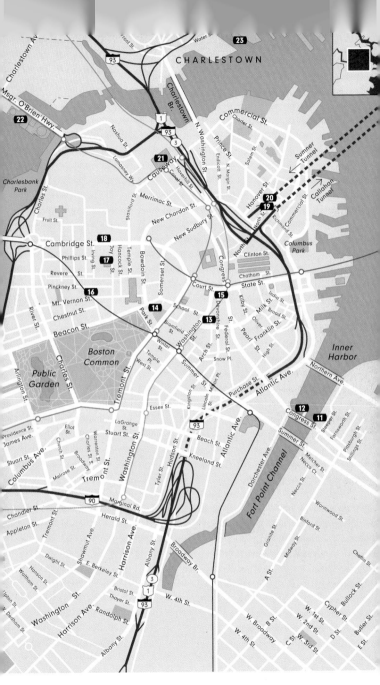

Listed by Site Number (cont.)

12 Boston Tea Party Museum

13 Old South Meeting House

14 Boston Athenaeum

15 Old State House

16 Nichols House

17 Mus of Afro-American History

18 Harrison Gray Otis House #1

19 Pierce-Hichborn Hse

20 Paul Revere House

21 Sports Museum of New England

22 Museum of Science/ Hayden Planetarium

23 USS *Constitution*

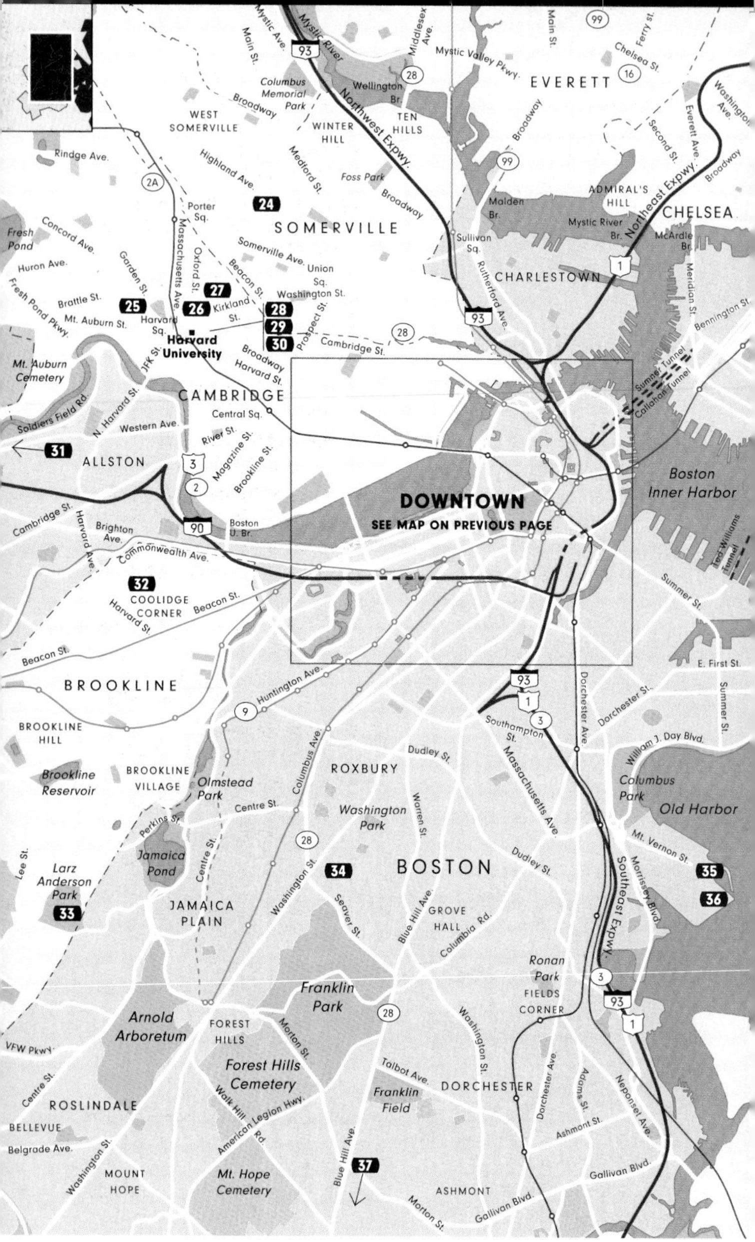

Listed by Site Number

24 Somerville Museum

25 Longfellow National Historic Site

26 Harvard Natural History Museums

27 Harvard Semitic Mus

28 Sackler Museum

29 Fogg Art Museum

30 Busch-Reisinger

31 DeCordova Museum

32 Kennedy National Historic Site

33 Museum of Transportation

34 Museum of Afro-American Artists

35 Kennedy Library

36 Commonwealth Mus

37 Blue Hills Trailside

Listed Alphabetically

Blue Hills Trailside, 37. 1904 Canton Ave, Milton ☎ 333-0690

Boston Athenaeum, 14. 10½ Beacon St ☎ 227-0270

Boston Public Library, 9. 666 Boylston St ☎ 536-5400

Boston Tea Party Museum, 12. Congress St Bridge ☎ 338-1773

Botanical Museum, 26. (*see* Harvard Natural History Museums)

Busch-Reisinger, 30. 32 Quincy St, Cam ☎ 495-9400

Children's Museum, 11. 300 Congress St ☎ 426-8855

Commonwealth Museum, 36. 220 Morrissey Blvd ☎ 727-9268

DeCordova Museum, 31. 51 Sandy Pond Rd, Lincoln ☎ 781/259-8355

Fogg Art Museum, 29. 32 Quincy St, Cam ☎ 495-9400

Gibson House, 10. 137 Beacon St ☎ 267-6338

Harrison Gray Otis House #1, 18. 141 Cambridge St ☎ 227-3956

Hart Nautical/MIT, 1. 77 Mass Ave, Cambridge ☎ 253-4444

Harvard Natural History Museums, 26 24 Oxford St, Cam ☎ 495-3045

Harvard Semitic Museum, 27. 6 Divinity St, Cam ☎ 495-4631

Hayden Planetarium, 22. Science Park ☎ 723-2500

Institute of Contemporary Art, 8. 955 Boylston St ☎ 266-5152

Isabella Stewart Gardner Museum, 4. 280 Fenway ☎ 566-1401

Kennedy Library, 35. Columbia Pt, Dorchester ☎ 929-4500

Kennedy National Historic Site, 32. 83 Beals St, Brookline ☎ 566-7937

List Visual Arts Center/MIT, 3. 20 Ames St, Cam ☎ 253-4680

Longfellow National Historic Site, 25. 105 Brattle St, Cam ☎ 876-4491

Longyear Museum & Historical Society, 6. 271 Huntington Ave, ☎ 267-6688

Mapparium/Christian Science, 7. Norway St & Mass Ave ☎ 450-2000

MIT Museum, 1. 265 Mass Ave, Cam ☎ 253-4444

Minerological & Geological Museum, 26. (*see* Harvard Natural History Museums)

Museum of Afro-Amer Artists, 34. 300 Walnut Ave, Roxbury ☎ 442-8614

Museum of Afro-American History, 17. 46 Joy St ☎ 742-1854

Museum of Fine Arts, 5. 465 Huntington Ave ☎ 267-9300

Museum of Science, 22. Science Park ☎ 723-2500

Museum of Transportation, 33. 15 Newton St, Brookline ☎ 522-6547

Museum of Zoology, 26. (*see* Harvard Natural History Museums)

Nichols House, 16. 55 Mt Vernon St ☎ 227-6993

Old South Meeting House, 13. 294 Washington St ☎ 482-6439

Old State House, 15. 206 Washington St ☎ 720-3290

Paul Revere House, 20. 19 North Square ☎ 523-2338

Peabody Museum, 26. (*see* Harvard Natural History Museums)

Pierce-Hichborn House, 19. 19 North Square ☎ 523-1676

Sackler Museum, 28. 485 Broadway at Quincy St, Cam ☎ 495-9400

Somerville Museum, 24. 1 Westwood Rd, Somerville ☎ 666-9810

Sports Museum of New England, 21. FleetCenter, Causeway St ☎ 624-1234

USS *Constitution*, 23. Constitution Wharf, Charlestown ☎ 242-5670

Listed by Site Number

1	MPG Gallery	8	Guild of Boston	12	Arden Gallery
2	Kanegis Gallery	9	Copley Society of Boston	12	Chase Gallery
3	Vose Galleries			13	Galerie Europeenne
4	Nielsen Gallery	9	Alfred Walker Fine Arts	13	Kelly Barrette Fine Arts
5	Society Arts & Crafts	10	Michalopoulos Gallery	14	Judi Rotenburg
6	Pucker Gallery	11	Dyansen	15	Haley & Steele
7	Childs Gallery				

Listed Alphabetically

Alfred Walker Fine Arts, 9. 158 Newbury St ☎ 247-1319

Alpha Gallery, 20. 14 Newbury St ☎ 536-4465

Arden Gallery, 12. 129 Newbury St ☎ 247-0610

Barbara Krakow Gallery, 21. 10 Newbury St ☎ 262-4490

Beth Urdang Gallery, 22. 1 Newbury St ☎ 424-8468

Chase Gallery, 12. 129 Newbury St ☎ 859-7222

Childs Gallery, 7. 169 Newbury St ☎ 266-1108

Copley Society of Boston, 9. 158 Newbury St ☎ 536-5049

Dyansen, 11. 132A Newbury St ☎ 262-4800

Galerie Europeenne, 13. 123 Newbury St ☎ 859-7062

Gallery Naga, 16. 67 Newbury St ☎ 267-9060

Guild of Boston Artists, 8. 162 Newbury St ☎ 536-7660

Haley & Steele, 15. 91 Newbury St ☎ 536-6339

Judi Rotenburg, 14. 130 Newbury St ☎ 437-1518

Kanegis Gallery, 2. 244 Newbury St ☎ 267-6735

Kelly Barrette Fine Arts, 13. 123 Newbury St ☎ 266-2475

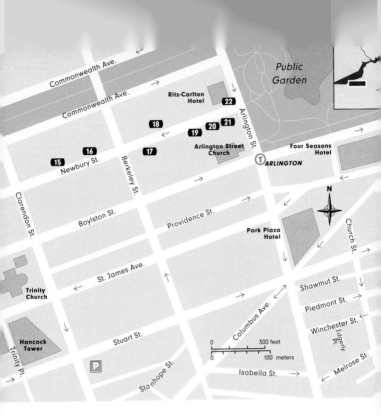

Listed by Site Number (cont.)

16 Gallery Naga
17 Robert Klein Gallery
18 Newbury Fine Arts
19 New England School
   of Art Design
20 Alpha Gallery

20 Miller Block Gallery
21 Barbara Krakow
   Gallery
22 Beth Urdang Gallery

Listed Alphabetically (cont.)

Michalopoulos Gallery, 10.
166 Newbury St ☎ 267-0202

Miller Block Gallery, 20.
14 Newbury St ☎ 536-4650

MPG Gallery, 1. 285 Newbury St
☎ 437-1596

Newbury Fine Arts, 18.
29 Newbury St ☎ 536-0210

**New England School of
Art Design, 19.**
28 Newbury St ☎ 536-0383

Nielsen Gallery, 4. 179 Newbury St
☎ 266-4835

Pucker Gallery, 6. 171 Newbury St
☎ 267-9473

Robert Klein Gallery, 17.
38 Newbury St ☎ 267-7997

Society of Arts & Crafts, 5.
175 Newbury St ☎ 266-1810

Vose Galleries, 3.
238 Newbury St ☎ 536-6176

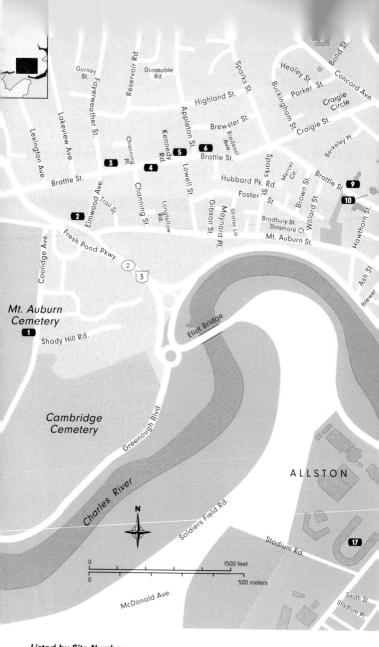

Listed by Site Number

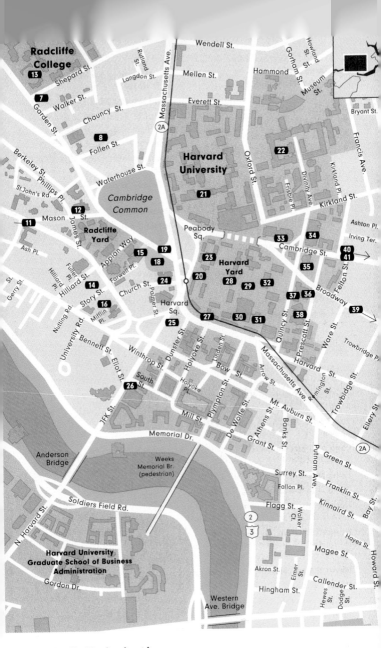

Listed by Site Number (cont.)

22 Harvard Museums of
Natural History

23 Holden Chapel

24 First Parish Church

25 Cambridge
Discovery

26 John Hicks House

27 Wadsworth House

28 University Hall

29 Harvard Yard

30 Widener Library

31 Pusey Library

32 Sever Hall

33 Memorial Hall/
Sanders Theater

34 Gund Hall

35 Arthur M. Sackler
Museum

36 Fogg Art Museum

37 Busch-Reisinger
Museum

38 Carpenter Visual Arts

39 Fuller House

40 Sacred Heart Church

41 St Francis of Assisi
Church

Listed Alphabetically

Arthur M. Sackler Museum, 35. 485 Broadway ☎ 495-9400

Asa Gray House, 7. 88 Garden St

Boylston Hall, 21. Harvard Yard

Brattle House, 16. 42 Brattle St ☎ 547-6789

Brattle Street (Tory Row), 4.

Busch-Reisinger Museum, 37. 32 Quincy St ☎ 495-9400

Cambridge Discovery Booth, 25. Zero Harvard Square ☎ 497-1630

Carpenter Visual Arts, 38. Prescott St

Christ Church, 15. Zero Garden St ☎ 876-0200

Dawes Island, 19. Garden St

Dexter Pratt House, 14. 56 Brattle St ☎ 547-6789

Elmwood House, 2. 33 Elmwood Ave

Fayerweather House, 3. 175 Brattle St

First Church Congregational, 12. 11 Garden St ☎ 547-2724

First Parish Church, 24. 3 Church St ☎ 876-7772

Fogg Art Museum, 36. 32 Quincy St ☎ 495-9400

Fuller House, 39. 71 Cherry St

Gund Hall, 34. Quincy St

Harvard Museums of Natural History, 22. 24 Oxford St ☎ 495-3045

Harvard Stadium, 17. N Harvard St & Soldiers Field Rd ☎ 495-2211

Harvard Yard, 29. Harvard Square

Holden Chapel, 23. Harvard Yard

Hooper House, 5. 159 Brattle St

John Hicks House, 26. 64 JFK St

Longfellow National Historic Site, 9. 105 Brattle St ☎ 876-4491

Massachusetts Hall, 20. Harvard Yard

Memorial Hall/Sanders Theater, 33. Harvard Yard

Mt Auburn Cemetery, 1. Mt Auburn St ☎ 547-7105

Old Burying Ground, 18. Massachusetts Ave & Church St ☎ 876-7772

Oliver Hastings House, 10. 101 Brattle St

Pusey Library, 31. Harvard Yard

Radcliffe College, 13. 10 Garden St ☎ 495-8600

Richards House, 8. 15 Follen St

Sacred Heart Church, 40. 49 Sixth St ☎ 547-0399

St Francis of Assisi Church, 41. 42 Sciarappa St ☎ 876-6754

Sever Hall, 32. Harvard Yard

Stoughton House, 11. 90 Brattle St

Thomas Lee House, 6. 153 Brattle St

University Hall, 28. Harvard Yard

Wadsworth House, 27. Massachusetts Ave & Holyoke St

Widener Library, 30. Harvard Yard ☎ 495-2413

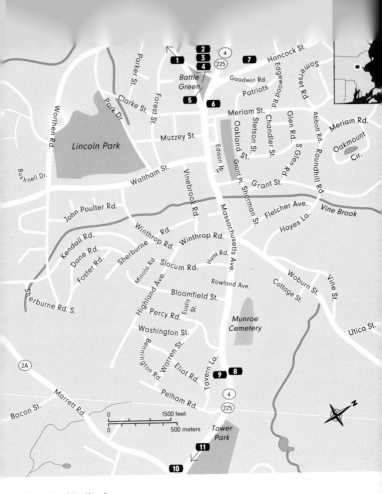

Listed by Site Number

1 Paul Revere Capture Site
2 Battle Green
3 Line of Battle Boulder
4 Revolutionary Monument
5 Minuteman Statue
6 Buckman Tavern
7 Hancock-Clarke House
8 Percy's Reinforcement Site
9 Munroe Tavern
10 Museum of our National Heritage
11 Old Schwamb Mill

Listed Alphabetically

Battle Green, 2. 1875 Mass Ave

Buckman Tavern, 6. I Bedford St ☎ 781/862-5598

Hancock-Clarke House, 7. 35 Hancock St ☎ 781/861-0928

Line of Battle Boulder, 3. Battle Green

Minuteman Statue, 5. Battle Green

Munroe Tavern, 9. 1332 Mass Ave ☎ 781/674-9238

Museum of Our National Heritage, 10. 33 Marrett Rd ☎ 781/861-6559

Old Schwamb Mill, 11. 17 Mill Lane, Arlington ☎ 781/643-0554

Paul Revere Capture Site, 1. Lexington Rd, Lincoln

Percy's Reinforcement Site, 8. Mass Ave opposite Munroe Tavern

Revolutionary Monument, 4. Battle Green

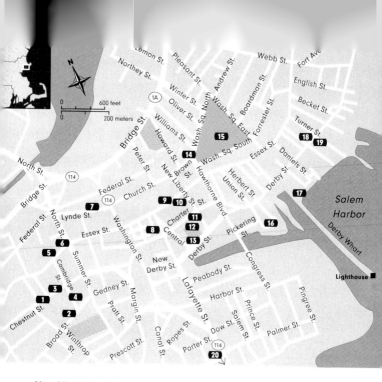

Listed by Site Number

1 Chestnut Street
2 Pickering House
3 Steven Phillips House
4 Hamilton Hall
5 First Church
6 Witch House
7 Witch Dungeon
8 Old Town Hall

9 National Park Visitors Center
10 Peabody Essex Mus
11 Witch Trials Memorial
12 Old Burying Point
13 Wax Museum
14 Salem Witch Museum

15 Salem Common
16 Pickering Wharf
17 Salem Maritime Site
18 Ye Olde Pepper Co
19 House of 7 Gables
20 Salem 1630 Pioneer Village

Listed Alphabetically

Chestnut Street, 1.

First Church, 5. 316 Essex St

Hamilton Hall, 4. 9 Chestnut St
☎ 978/744-0805

House of Seven Gables, 19.
54 Turner St ☎ 978/744-0991

National Park Visitors Center, 9.
Museum Place ☎ 978/740-1650

Old Burying Point, 12. Charter St

Old Town Hall, 8. Derby Sq

Peabody Essex Museum, 10.
East India Sq ☎ 978/745-9500

Pickering House, 2. 18 Broad St
☎ 978/744-1647

Pickering Wharf, 16. Derby St
☎ 978/740-6990

Salem Common, 15. Washington Sq

Salem Maritime Site, 17.
174 Derby St ☎ 978/740-1650

Salem 1630 Pioneer Village, 20.
Route IA ☎ 978/744-0991

Salem Witch Museum, 14.
Washington Sq N ☎ 978/744-1692

Stephen Phillips House, 3.
34 Chestnut St ☎ 978/744-0440

Wax Museum, 13. 288 Derby St
☎ 978/740-2929

Witch Dungeon, 7. 16 Lynde St
☎ 978/741-3570

Witch House, 6. 9 North St
☎ 978/744-0180

Witch Trials Memorial, 11. Charter St

Ye Olde Pepper Co, 18. 122 Derby St
☎ 978/745-2744

Listed by Site Number

1 Thoreau Lyceum
2 Old North Bridge
3 Old Manse
4 Bullet Hole House
5 Sleepy Hollow Cemetery
6 Colonial Inn

7 Monument Square
8 Wright Tavern
9 First Parish Church
10 Old Hill Burying Ground
11 Hartwell Tavern
12 Emerson House

13 Concord Museum
14 Orchard House
15 The Wayside Tavern
16 Grapevine Cottage
17 Thoreau's Cabin Site
18 Meriam's Corner
19 Battle Rd Visitors Ctr

Listed Alphabetically

Battle Road Visitors Center, 19.
Rt 2A, Lexington ☎ 781/862-7753

Bullet Hole House, 4.
Monument St

Colonial Inn, 6. 48 Monument Sq
☎ 978/369-9200

Concord Chamber of Commerce, 8.
2 Lexington Rd ☎ 978/369-9602

Concord Museum, 13.
200 Lexington Rd ☎ 978/369-9609

Emerson House, 12. 28 Cambridge
Tnpk ☎ 978/369-2236

First Parish Church, 9. 20 Lexington
Rd ☎ 978/369-9602

Grapevine Cottage, 16.
491 Lexington Rd

Hartwell Tavern, 11. Lexington Rd

Meriam's Corner, 18. Lexington Rd

Monument Square, 7. Main St

Old Hill Burying Ground, 10.
Lexington Rd

Old Manse, 3. Monument St
☎ 978/369-3909

Old North Bridge, 2.
174 Liberty St

Orchard House, 14.
399 Lexington Rd ☎ 978/369-4118

Sleepy Hollow Cemetery, 5.
Rt 62W

Thoreau's Cabin Site, 17.
Walden Pond, Rt 126

Thoreau Lyceum, 1. 156 Belknap St,
☎ 978/369-5912

The Wayside Tavern, 15.
455 Lexington Rd ☎ 978/369-6975

**Wright Tavern/Chamber of
Commerce, 8.** 2 Lexington Rd
☎ 978/369-9602

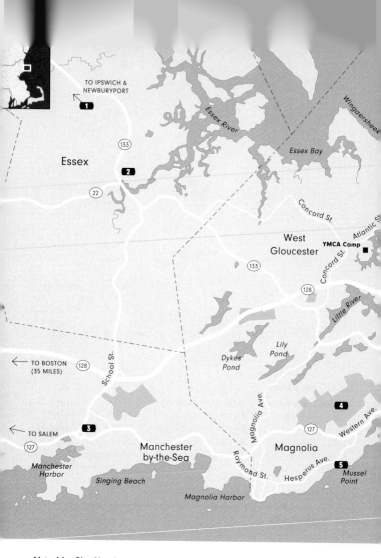

Essex

133

22

Essex River

Essex Bay

Concord St.

West Gloucester

YMCA Camp

Atlantic St

Wingaersheek

133

128

Concord St.

Little River

TO BOSTON (35 MILES)

128

School St.

Dykes Pond

Lily Pond

Magnolia Ave.

4

Western Ave.

TO SALEM

127

3

Manchester Harbor

Manchester by-the-Sea

Singing Beach

Raymond St.

Magnolia Harbor

127

Magnolia

Hesperus Ave.

5

Mussel Point

TO IPSWICH & NEWBURYPORT

1

Listed by Site Number

1 Castle Hill/Crane's Beach
2 Essex Shipbuilding Museum

3 Trask House
4 Ravenswood Park
5 Hammond Castle
6 Beauport Museum

7 Rocky Neck Art Colony
8 Gloucester Stage Company

Listed Alphabetically

Bearskin Neck, 15. Rockport

Beauport Museum, 6. 75 Eastern Point Rd, Gloucester ☎ 978/283-0800

Cape Ann Historical Society, 11. 27 Pleasant St, Gloucester ☎ 978/283-0455

Castle Hill/Crane's Beach, 1. 200 Argilla Rd, Ipswich ☎ 978/356-4354

Chamber Music Festival, 14. performs at 12 Main St (Rockport Art Assn), Rockport ☎ 978/546-7391

Essex Shipbuilding Museum, 2. 28 Main St, Essex ☎ 978/768-7541

Fishermen's Memorial, 9. Stacy Blvd, Gloucester

Gloucester Stage Co. 8. 267 E Main St, Gloucester ☎ 978/281-4099

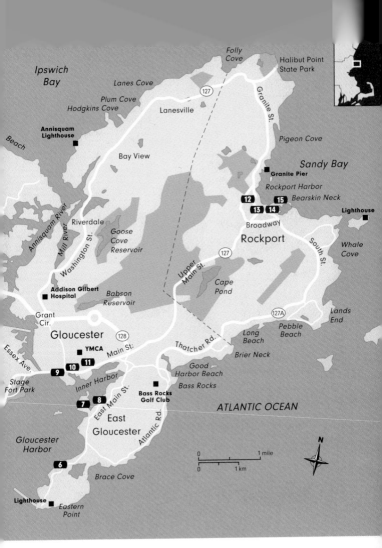

Listed by Site Number (cont.)

9 Fishermen's Memorial

10 Sargent House Museum

11 Cape Ann Historical Society

12 Sandy Bay Museum

13 Toad Hall Book Store

14 Chamber Music Festival

15 Bearskin Neck

Listed Alphabetically (cont.)

Hammond Castle Museum, 5.
80 Hesperus Ave, Gloucester
☎ 978/283-2080

Ravenswood Park, 4.
Western Ave, Gloucester

Rocky Neck Art Colony, 7.
East Gloucester

Sandy Bay Historical Society, 12.
40 King St, Rockport ☎ 978/546-9533

Sargent House Museum, 10.
49 Middle St, Gloucester
☎ 978/281-2432

Toad Hall Book Store, 13.
51 Main St, Rockport ☎ 978/546-7323

Trask House, 3. 10 Union St,
Manchester-by-the-Sea
☎ 978/526-7230

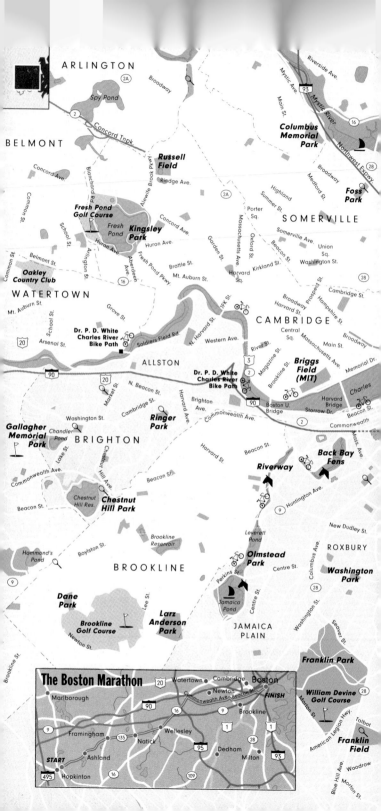

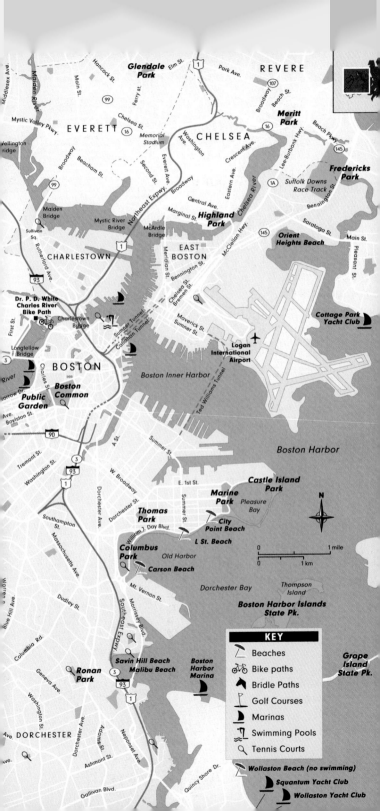

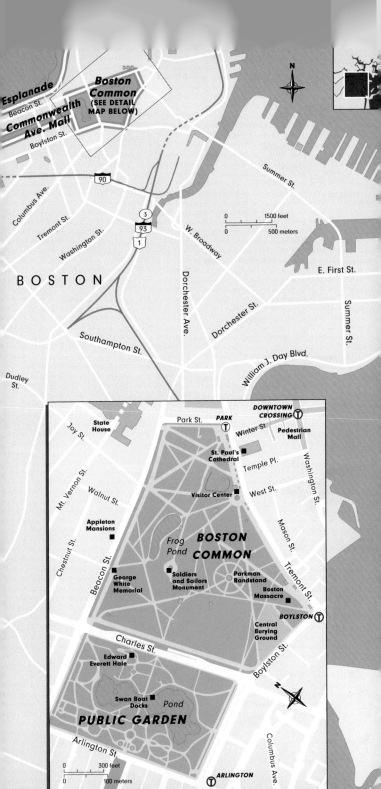

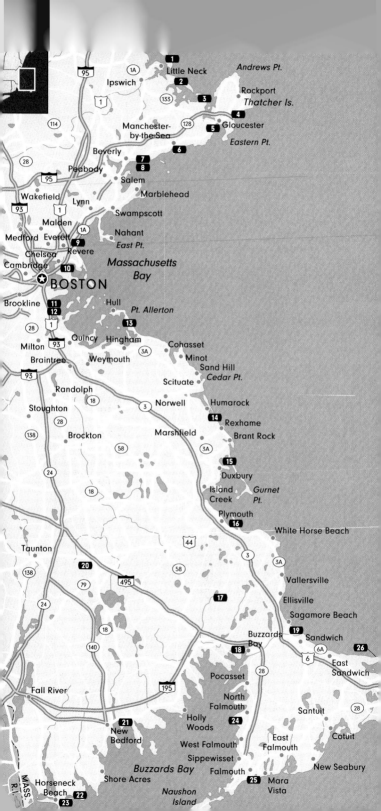

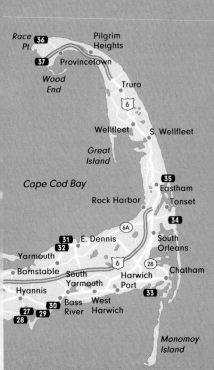

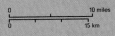

0   10 miles
0   15 km

N

ATLANTIC OCEAN

Race Pt. **36**
Pilgrim Heights
37 Provincetown
Wood End
Truro
6
Wellfleet   S. Wellfleet
Great Island
Cape Cod Bay
Rock Harbor
35 Eastham
Tonset
6A
34
E. Dennis
31
32
Yarmouth
South Orleans
Barnstable
South Yarmouth
6
Harwich Port
28
Chatham
Hyannis
30
Bass River
West Harwich
33
27 **29**
28
Monomoy Island
Nantucket Sound

Listed Alphabetically

NORTH SHORE

Crane's Beach, 2. Ipswich
R,L,F,P

Cressy Beach, 5. Stage Fort Pk,
Gloucester ☎ 978/281-9790. *R*

Dane St, 7. Beverly
☎ 978/921-6067. *R,L,P*

Good Harbor, 4. Thatcher Rd,
Gloucester ☎ 978/281-9790. *R,L,F,P*

Lynch Park, 8. Ober St, Beverly
☎ 978/921-6067. *L,P*

Plum Island, 1. Newburyport
☎ 978/462-6680. *R,L*

Singing Beach, 6.
Manchester-by-the-Sea. *R,L*

Wingaersheek, 3. Concord St,
Gloucester ☎ 978/281-9790. *R,L,F,P*

GREATER BOSTON

Constitution Beach, 10. E Boston
☎ 727-5114. *R,L,F,P*

Malibu Beach, 11. Dorchester
☎ 727-5114. *R,L,F,P*

Revere Beach, 9. Rt 1A,
Revere ☎ 781/286-8190. *R,L,F,P*

Savin Hill Beach, 12.
Dorchester ☎ 727-5114. *R,L,F,P*

SOUTH SHORE

College/Fearing Ponds, 17.
Plymouth ☎ 508/866-2526. *R,P*

Duxbury Beach, 15. Duxbury
☎ 781/934-6586. *R,L,F,P*

Humarock Beach, 14. Marshfield
☎ 781/545-8740. *R,L*

Nantasket Beach, 13. Hull
☎ 781/925-2000. *R,L,F,P*

Onset Beach, 18. Wareham
☎ 508/291-3101. *F,P*

Plymouth Beach, 16. Plymouth
☎ 800/872-1620. *L,F,P*

Scusset Beach, 19. Bourne
☎ 508/888-0859. *R,F,P*

BRISTOL COUNTY

Demarest Lloyd State Park, 22.
Dartmouth ☎ 508/636-3298. *R,L*

Fort Phoenix State Park, 21.
Fairhaven ☎ 508/992-4524. *R,L*

Horseneck Beach, 23. Westport
☎ 508/636-8816. *R,L*

Massasoit State Park, 20. E Taunton
☎ 508/822-7405. *R,L*

CAPE COD

Bass River Beach, 30. So Shore Dr,
Yarmouth ☎ 508/398-2231. *R,F,P*

Coast Guard Beach, 35.
Rt 6, Eastham ☎ 508/255-3421. *R,F,P*

Corporation Rd Beach, 31.
Rt 6A, Dennis ☎ 508/394-8300. *R,F,P*

Harding's Beach, 33. Rt 28,
W Chatham ☎ 508/945-5158. *R,F*

Herring Cove, 37. Rt 6, Provincetown
☎ 508/487-7097. *R,F,P*

Kalmus Park, 27. Ocean St, Hyannis
☎ 508/790-6345. *R,F,P*

Mayflower Beach, 32. Rt 6A, Dennis
☎ 508/394-8300. *R,F,P*

Nauset Beach, 34. Rt 28, E Orleans
☎ 508/240-3785. *R,F,P*

Old Silver, 24. Quaker Rd,
No Falmouth ☎ 508/457-2567. *R,F,P*

Orrin Keyes, 28. Sea St, Hyannis
☎ 508/790-6345. *R,F,P*

Race Point, 36. Rt 6, Provincetown
☎ 508/487-7097. *R*

Sandy Neck, 26. Rt 6A, W Barnstable
☎ 508/790-6345. *R,F,P*

Sea Gull, 29. South Sea Ave,
W Yarmouth ☎ 508/398-2231. *R,F,P*

Surf Drive, 25. Surf Dr, Falmouth
☎ 508/457-2567. *R,F,P*

*Note: Hours for lifeguards and
refreshments are limited; call
to check.*

R=Restrooms L=Lifeguard F=Food P=Parking

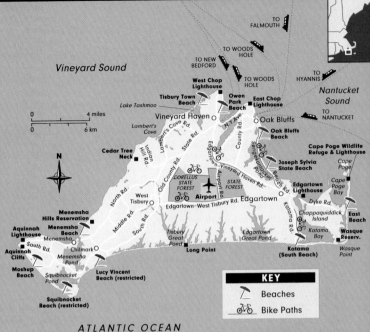

Martha's Vineyard

TO FALMOUTH

TO WOODS HOLE

TO NEW BEDFORD

TO WOODS HOLE

TO HYANNIS

Nantucket Sound

TO NANTUCKET

Vineyard Sound

West Chop Lighthouse

Tisbury Town Beach

Lake Tashmoo

Owen Park Beach

East Chop Lighthouse

Vineyard Haven

Oak Bluffs

Lambert's Cove

Oak Bluffs Beach

Cedar Tree Neck

Lambert's Cove Rd.

State Rd.

County Rd.

N.T. Ave.

Cape Poge Wildlife Refuge & Lighthouse

Joseph Sylvia State Beach

Old County Rd.

Indian Hill Rd.

Airport Rd.

Vineyard Haven Rd.

Sengekontacket Pond

State Beach Rd.

Edgartown Lighthouse

Cape Poge

Cape Poge Bay

North Rd.

CORELLUS STATE FOREST

STATE FOREST

West Tisbury

Airport

Edgartown-West Tisbury Rd.

Edgartown

Katama Rd.

Dyke Rd.

Chappaquiddick Island

East Beach

Menemsha Hills Reservation

Middle Rd.

South Rd.

Tisbury Great Pond

Edgartown Great Pond

Wasque Reserv.

Aquinnah Lighthouse

Menemsha Beach

Menemsha

Chilmark

Long Point

Katama Bay

Wasque Point

Aquinnah Cliffs

South Rd.

Menemsha Pond

Katama (South Beach)

Moshup Beach

Squibnocket Pond

Lucy Vincent Beach (restricted)

Squibnocket Beach (restricted)

ATLANTIC OCEAN

N

0 — 4 miles
0 — 6 km

KEY

Beaches

Bike Paths

Nantucket

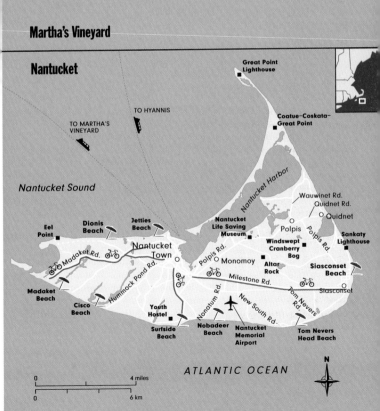

Great Point Lighthouse

TO HYANNIS

Coatue-Coskata-Great Point

TO MARTHA'S VINEYARD

Nantucket Sound

Nantucket Harbor

Wauwinet Rd.
Quidnet Rd.

Quidnet

Eel Point

Dionis Beach

Jetties Beach

Nantucket Life Saving Museum

Polpis

Polpis Rd.

Sankaty Lighthouse

Madaket Rd.

Nantucket Town

Windswept Cranberry Bog

Polpis Rd.

Monomoy

Altar Rock

Siasconset Beach

Hummock Pond Rd.

Madaket Beach

Cisco Beach

Youth Hostel

Milestone Rd.

Siasconset

Tom Nevers Rd.

Surfside Beach

Nobadeer Beach

Nonantum Rd.

Nantucket Memorial Airport

New South Rd.

Tom Nevers Head Beach

ATLANTIC OCEAN

N

0 — 4 miles
0 — 6 km

Foxboro Access

Dorchester Bay

BOSTON

135
27   16
Needham
EXIT 17
EXIT 16
Dedham
Milton
Islington
EXIT 15
EXIT 1
Westwood   109
28
Holliston
115
Medfield   1A
Norwood   EXIT 2   EXIT 4 / EXIT 21
16
Millis   27
Canton
109
EXIT 20
N
Walpole   EXIT 10
Norfolk   EXIT 9   Sharon
115   Stoughton
Foxboro Stadium   EXIT 8
EXIT 18
Franklin   1A
EXIT 17   Foxboro   138
140   1
495   EXIT 17
Wrentham   95   EXIT 7
EXIT 14   EXIT 18
121   EXIT 15   EXIT 6 / EXIT 13   Easton
106   EXIT 16
Mansfield
R.I.

0   4 miles
0   6 km

93
95   128
1
28
93
28
24
1A
95
27
1
24

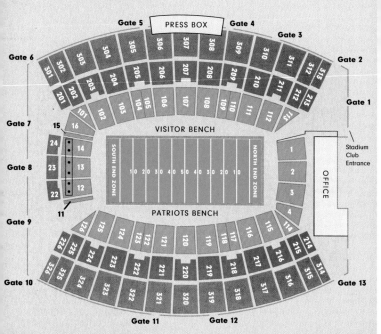

Foxboro Stadium

Gate 5   PRESS BOX   Gate 4
Gate 6   Gate 3
Gate 2

304 305 306 307 308 309 310 311 312 313
301 302 303 204 205 206 207 208 209 210 211 212 213
201 202 203 204 105 106 107 108 109 110 111 112 113
101 102 103 104 105 106 107 108 109 110 111 112 113

Gate 1

15 16
Gate 7
24 14
23 13   VISITOR BENCH
22 12   SOUTH END ZONE   10 20 30 40 50 40 30 20 10   NORTH END ZONE
11   PATRIOTS BENCH

Gate 8
Gate 9

1
2
3
4

Stadium Club Entrance
OFFICE

126 125 124 123 122 121 120 119 118 117 116 115 114
226 225 224 223 222 221 220 219 218 217 216 215 214
326 325 324 323 322 321 320 319 318 317 316 315 314

Gate 10
Gate 11   Gate 12
Gate 13

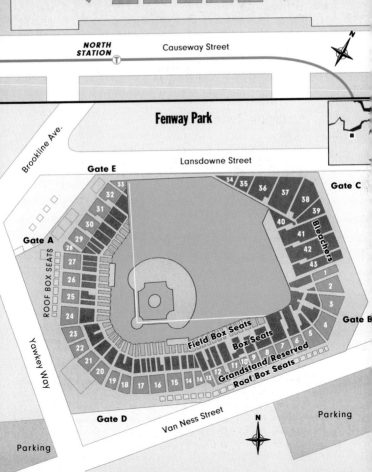

FleetCenter

314 315 316 317 318
319 320
137 139 141 143 145
147 149
10 11 12 13 14
15
312 313
133 135
9a/9b
151 153 321
322
311 131
129
8
16
310
127 7
17 155 323
309
125 6
18 157 324
308
123 121
5
19 159 325
307
119 117
4
20
101 103 326
306
3 2 1 22 21
105 327
305 115 113 111 109 107
328
304 303 302 301 330 329

NORTH STATION (T) Causeway Street

N

Fenway Park

Brookline Ave.

Lansdowne Street

Gate E

Gate C

33 34 35 36 37 38
32 39
31 40
30 41
29 Bleachers
28 42
Gate A 27 43
26 1
ROOF BOX SEATS 25 2
24 3
23 Gate B
22 4
21 Field Box Seats
20 Box Seats 5
19 18 17 16 15 14 13 12 11 10 9 8 7 6
Grandstand/Reserved
Roof Box Seats

Yawkey Way

Gate D Van Ness Street N Parking

Parking

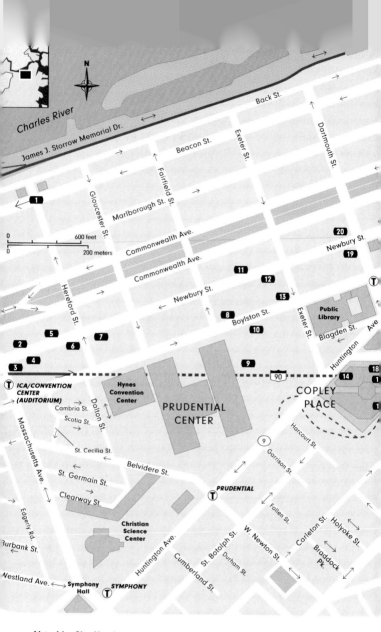

Listed by Site Number

1	Barnes & Noble at BU	**11**	London Lace	**18**	Gucci
2	Urban Outfitters	**12**	Emporio Armani	**18**	Louis Vuitton
3	Tower Records	**13**	Restoration Hardware	**19**	Alianza
4	Trident Bookseller	**14**	Bally	**20**	Kitchen Arts
5	Jasmine/Sola	**14**	Tiffany & Co	**21**	Loulou's Lost & Found
6	Mystery Train	**14**	Victoria's Secret	**22**	Pottery Barn
7	John Fluevog Shoes	**15**	Jaeger	**23**	Betsey Jenney
8	Crate & Barrel	**16**	Neiman Marcus	**24**	Bellezza Home and Garden
9	Saks Fifth Ave	**17**	The Sharper Image	**24**	Pratesi
10	Lord & Taylor	**17**	Joan & David		

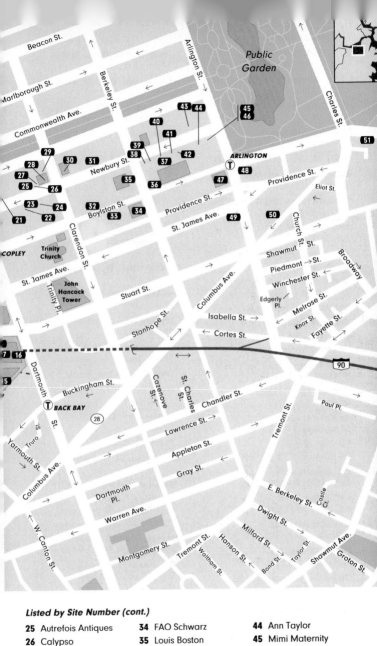

Listed by Site Number (cont.)

25 Autrefois Antiques	34 FAO Schwarz	44 Ann Taylor
26 Calypso	35 Louis Boston	45 Mimi Maternity
27 Pierre Deux	36 Jos A Bank Clothiers	46 Burberrys Ltd
28 Cole Haan	37 Gianni Versace	47 Shreve, Crump & Low
29 OKW	38 Brooks Brothers	48 Hermes
30 John Lewis	39 Cartier	49 Laura Ashley
31 Eye of the Needle	40 Alan Bilzerian	50 LJ Peretti & Co
32 Willowbee & Kent	41 Dorfman Jewelers	51 Repertoire
33 Globe Corner Bookstore	42 Giorgio Armani	
	43 Domain	

Listed Alphabetically

Alan Bilzerian, 40.
34 Newbury St ☎ 536-1001

Alianza, 19. 154 Newbury St
☎ 262-2385

Ann Taylor, 44. 18 Newbury St
☎ 262-0763

Autrefois Antiques, 25.
125 Newbury St ☎ 424-8823

Bally, 14. Copley Place ☎ 437-1910

Barnes & Noble at BU, 1.
660 Beacon St ☎ 267-8484

Bellezza Home and Garden, 24.
129 Newbury St ☎ 266-1183

Betsey Jenney, 23. 114 Newbury St
☎ 536-2610

Brooks Brothers, 38. 46 Newbury St
☎ 267-2600

Burberrys Ltd, 46. 2 Newbury St
☎ 236-1000

Calypso, 26. 115 Newbury St ☎ 421-1887

Cartier, 39. 40 Newbury St ☎ 262-3300

Cole Haan, 28. 109 Newbury St
☎ 536-7826

Crate & Barrel, 8. 777 Boylston St
☎ 262-8700

Domain, 43. 7 Newbury St
☎ 266-5252

Dorfman Jewelers, 41.
24 Newbury St ☎ 536-2022

Emporio Armani, 12.
210 Newbury St ☎ 262-7300

Eye of the Needle, 31.
85 Newbury St ☎ 859-7999

FAO Schwarz, 34.
440 Boylston St ☎ 266-5101

Gianni Versace, 37.
12 Newbury St ☎ 536-8300

Giorgio Armani, 42.
22 Newbury St ☎ 267-3200

Globe Corner Bookstore, 33.
500 Boylston St ☎ 859-8008

Gucci, 18. Copley Place ☎ 247-3000

Hermes, 48. 22 Arlington St ☎ 482-8707

Jaeger, 15. 4 Copley Place ☎ 437-1163

Jasmine/Sola, 5. 329-333-344
Newbury St ☎ 437-8466

Joan & David, 17. 2 Copley Place
☎ 536-0600

John Fluevog Shoes, 7. 302 Newbury
St ☎ 266-1079

John Lewis, 30. 97 Newbury St
☎ 266-6665

Jos A Bank Clothiers, 35. 399
Boylston St ☎ 536-5050

Kitchen Arts, 20. 161 Newbury St
☎ 266-8701

LJ Peretti & Co, 50. Park Square
☎ 482-0218

Laura Ashley, 49. 75 Arlington St
☎ 357-5151

London Lace, 11. 215 Newbury St
☎ 267-3506

Lord & Taylor, 10. 760 Boylston St
☎ 262-6000

Loulou's Lost & Found, 20.
121 Newbury St ☎ 859-8593

Louis Boston, 35. 234 Berkeley St
☎ 262-6100

Louis Vuitton, 18. Copley Place
☎ 437-6519

Mimi Maternity, 45. 10 Newbury St
☎ 262-8012

Mystery Train, 6. 306 Newbury St
☎ 536-0216

Neiman Marcus, 16. 5 Copley Place
☎ 536-3660

OKW, 29. 234 Clarendon St ☎ 266-4114

Pierre Deux, 27. 111 Newbury St
☎ 536-6364

Pottery Barn, 22. 122 Newbury St
☎ 266-6553

Pratesi, 24. 110 Newbury St ☎ 262-5998

Repertoire, 51. 114 Boylston St
☎ 426-3865

Restoration Hardware, 13. 711
Boylston St ☎ 578-0088

Saks Fifth Ave, 9. Prudential Center
☎ 262-8500

Shreve, Crump & Low, 47.
330 Boylston St ☎ 267-9100

The Sharper Image, 17.
Copley Place ☎ 262-7010

Tiffany & Co, 14. Copley Place
☎ 353-0222

Tower Records, 3. 360 Newbury St
☎ 247-5900

Trident Bookseller and Café, 4. 338
Newbury St ☎ 267-8688

Urban Outfitters, 2.
361 Newbury St ☎ 236-0088

Victoria's Secret, 14. Copley Place
☎ 266-7505

Willowbee & Kent Travel Co., 32.
519 Boylston St ☎ 437-6700

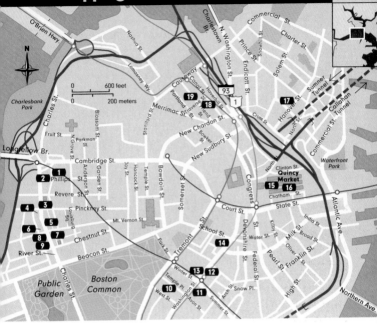

Listed by Site Number

1 Judith Dowling
2 Savenor's
3 Boston Antique Coop
4 Helen's Leather Shop
5 Upstairs Downstairs
6 Eugene Galleries
7 Devonia

8 Koo de Kir
9 Flat of the Hill
10 Brattle Bookshop
11 Macy's
12 Filene's Basement
13 Barnes & Noble
14 Borders

15 April Cornell
15 Bill Rodgers Running Center
16 Crate & Barrel
17 Mike's Pastry
18 Boomerangs
19 Hilton's Tent City

Listed Alphabetically

Barnes & Noble, 13.
395 Washington St ☎ 426–5184

Boston Antique Coop, 3.
119 Charles St ☎ 227–9810

Brattle Bookshop, 10.
9 West St ☎ 542–0210

Boomerangs, 18.
60 Canal St ☎ 723–2666

Borders, 14. 10–24 School St
☎ 557–7188

April Cornell, 15. Quincy Market
☎ 242–0280

Crate & Barrel, 16. Quincy Market
☎ 742–6025

Bill Rodgers Running Center, 15.
Quincy Market ☎ 723–5612

Devonia: Antiques for Dining, 7.
43 Charles St ☎ 523–8313

Eugene Galleries, 6.
76 Charles St ☎ 227–3062

Filene's Basement, 12.
426 Washington St ☎ 542–2011

Flat of the Hill, 9.
60 Charles St ☎ 619–9977

Helen's Leather Shop, 4.
110 Charles St ☎ 742–2077

Hilton's Tent City, 19.
272 Friend St ☎ 227–9242

Judith Dowling Asian Art, 1.
133 Charles St ☎ 523–5211

Koo de Kir, 8. 34 Charles St
☎ 723–8111

Mike's Pastry, 17.
300 Hanover St ☎ 742–3050

Macy's, 11. 450 Washington St
☎ 357–3000

Savenor's, 2. 160 Charles St
☎ 723–6328

Upstairs Downstairs, 5. 93 Charles
St ☎ 367–1950

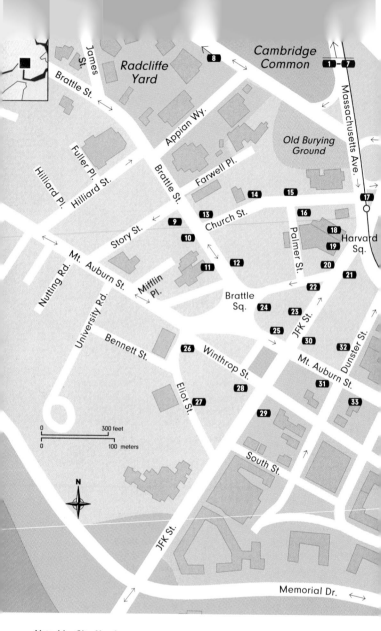

Listed by Site Number

1 Consignment Galleries
2 Irish Imports
3 Pepperweed
4 Kate's Mystery Books
5 Nomad
6 Abodeon
7 Marathon Sports
8 Hi-Rise Bread Co

9 Crate & Barrel
10 Utrecht Art Supplies
11 HMV
12 Jasmine/Sola
13 Hartnett's
14 Cambridge Artists' Coop
15 Beadworks
16 Globe Corner Bookstore

17 Out-of-Town News
18 The Body Shop
19 Harvard Coop
20 Cardullo's
21 Abercrombie & Fitch
22 Curious George Goes to WordsWorth
23 Urban Outfitters
24 WordsWorth

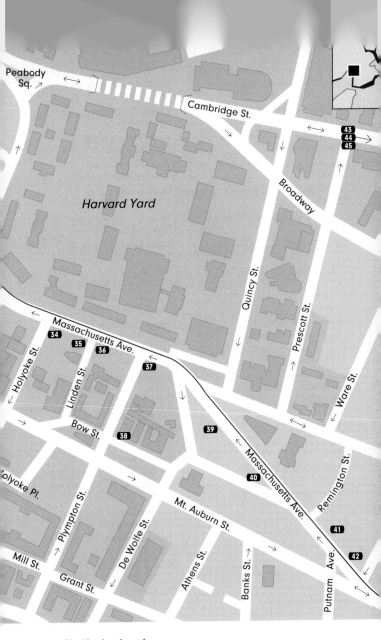

Listed by Site Number (cont.)

25 Tower Records	**32** Herrell's	**40** Mystery Train
26 Funny Farm	**33** Schoenhof's	**41** Games People Play
26 Second Time Around	Foreign Books	**42** Bowl & Board
27 New England	**34** J August	**43** New Words
Comics	**35** Leavitt & Peirce	**44** Garment District
28 Alpha Omega	**36** Bob Slate	**45** Rosie's Bakery
Jewelers	**37** Harvard Bookstore	
29 Harvard Shop	**38** Grolier Poetry Book	
30 Newbury Comics	Shop	
31 J Press	**39** Serendipity	

Listed Alphabetically

Abercrombie & Fitch, 21.
6 JFK St ☎ 354-8604

Abodeon, 6. 1731 Mass Ave
☎ 497-0137

Alpha Omega Jewelers, 28.
57 JFK St ☎ 864-1227

Beadworks, 15. 23 Church St
☎ 868-9777

Bob Slate, 36. 1288 Mass Ave
☎ 547-1230

The Body Shop, 18. 1440 Mass Ave
☎ 876-6334

Bowl & Board, 42. 1063 Mass Ave
☎ 661-0350

Cambridge Artists' Coop, 14.
59A Church St ☎ 868-4434

Cardullo's, 20. 6 Brattle St
☎ 491-8888

Consignment Galleries, 1.
2044 Mass Ave ☎ 354-4408

Crate & Barrel, 9. 48 Brattle St
☎ 876-6300

**Curious George Goes to
WordsWorth, 22.** 1 JFK St
☎ 498-0062

Funny Farm, 26. 8 Eliot St
☎ 661-3999

Games People Play, 41.
1105 Mass Ave ☎ 492-0711

The Garment District, 44.
200 Broadway ☎ 876-9795

Globe Corner Bookstore, 16.
28 Church St ☎ 497-6277

Grolier Poetry Book Shop, 38.
6 Plympton St ☎ 547-4648

Harnett's, 13. 47 Brattle St
☎ 491-4747

Harvard Bookstore, 37.
1256 Mass Ave ☎ 661-1515

Harvard Coop, 19.
1400 Mass Ave ☎ 499-2000

Harvard Shop, 29.
52 JFK St ☎ 576-3818

Herrell's, 32. 15 Dunster St
☎ 497-2179

Hi-Rise Bread Co, 8.
208 Concord Ave ☎ 876-8766

HMV, 11. 1 Brattle Sq
☎ 868-9696

Irish Imports, 2. 1735 Mass Ave
☎ 354-2511

J August, 34. 1320 Mass Ave
☎ 864-6650

Jasmine/Sola, 12. 37 Brattle St
☎ 354-6043

J Press, 31. 82 Mt Auburn St
☎ 547-9886

Kate's Mystery Books, 4.
2211 Mass Ave ☎ 491-2660

Leavitt & Peirce, 35.
1316 Mass Ave ☎ 547-0576

Marathon Sports, 7.
1654 Mass Ave ☎ 354-4161

Mystery Train, 40. 1208 Mass Ave
☎ 497-4024

New England Comics, 27.
14/A Eliot St ☎ 354-5352

New Words, 43.
186 Hampshire St ☎ 876-5310

Newbury Comics, 30.
36 JFK St ☎ 491-0337

Nomad, 5. 1741 Mass Ave
☎ 497-6677

Out-of-Town News, 17. Harvard Sq
☎ 354-7777

Pepperweed, 3.
1684 Mass Ave ☎ 547-7561

Rosie's Bakery, 45.
243 Hampshire St ☎ 491-9488

Schoenhof's Foreign Books, 33.
76A Mt Auburn St ☎ 547-8855

Second Time Around, 26.
8 Eliot St ☎ 491-7185

Serendipity, 39. 1312 Mass Ave
☎ 661-7143

Tower Records, 25.
95 Mt Auburn St ☎ 876-3377

Urban Outfitters, 23.
11 JFK St ☎ 864-0070

Utrecht Art Supplies, 10.
44 Brattle St ☎ 495-0250

WordsWorth, 24.
30 Brattle St ☎ 354-5201

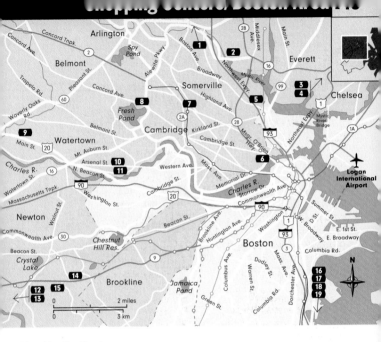

Listed by Site Number

1 Burlington Mall
2 Meadow Glen Mall
3 Liberty Tree Mall
4 Northshore Mall
5 Assembly Square Mall
6 Cambridgeside Galleria
7 Porter Square Arcade
8 Fresh Pond Shop Ctr
9 Colonial Mall
10 Watertown Mall
11 Arsenal Mall
12 Natick Mall
13 Shoppers' World
14 Chestnut Hill Mall
15 Atrium Mall
16 Emerald Sq Mall
17 Harbor Light Mall
18 South Shore Plaza
19 Hanover Mall

Listed Alphabetically

Arsenal Mall, 11. 485 Arsenal St, Watertown ☎ 923-4700

Assembly Square Mall, 5. 133 Middlesex Ave, Somerville ☎ 628-3800

Atrium Mall, 15. 300 Boylston St, Chestnut Hill ☎ 527-1400

Burlington Mall, 1. Rt 128, Burlington ☎ 781/272-8667

Cambridgeside Galleria, 6. 100 Cambridgeside Pl, Cam ☎ 621-8666

Chestnut Hill Mall, 14. 199 Boylston St, Newton ☎ 965-3037

Colonial Mall, 9. 85 River St, Waltham ☎ 781/899-3749

Emerald Square Mall, 16. Rt 1, No Attleboro ☎ 508/699-7979

Fresh Pond Shopping Center, 8. 186 Alewife Pkwy, Cam ☎ 491-4431

Hanover Mall, 19. Rt 53, Hanover ☎ 781/826-4392

Harbor Light Mall, 17. 789 Bridge St, Weymouth ☎ 781/335-3395

Liberty Tree Mall, 3. Rt 128, Danvers ☎ 978/777-0794

Meadow Glen Mall, 2. 3850 Mystic Valley Pkwy, Medford ☎ 781/395-1010

Natick Mall, 12. Rt 9, Natick ☎ 508/655-4800

Northshore Mall, 4. Rts 128 & 114, Peabody ☎ 978/531-3440

Porter Square Arcade, 7. 1 Porter Sq, Cambridge ☎ 576-2939

Shoppers' World, 13. Rts 9 & 30, Framingham ☎ 508/872-1257

South Shore Plaza, 18. 250 Granite St, Braintree ☎ 781/843-8200

Watertown Mall, 10. 550 Arsenal St, Watertown ☎ 926-4123

North End

SOMERVILLE

Old North Church

HAYMARKET T

Charles River

James J. Storrow Memorial Drive

Prudential Center

Copley Place

Christian Science Center

Symphony Hall

Northeastern University

Back Bay Fens Park

Fenway Park

Museum of Fine Arts

Briggs Field (MIT)

Waterfront Park

Summer Tunnel

Callahan Tunnel

Fitzgerald Expwy

Streets (North End): Prince St., Hull St., Sheafe St., Salem St., Charter St., Tileston St., Unity St., N. Bennet St., Hanover St., Hanover Ave., Battery St., Salutation St., Harris St., Clark St., Commercial St., Murphy Ct., Fleet St., North St., Lewis St., Sun Ct., Garden Ct., Richmond St., Fulton St., Commercial Wharf N., Noyes Pl., Baldwin Pl., Margaret St., Snowhill St., Thatcher St., Lombard Pl., Endicott St., Cooper St., Lynn St., Margin St., Stillman St., Morton St., Cross St., Blackstone St., Hanover St., Salt La., N. Union St., Creek Sq., Clinton St., New Sudbury St., Congress St.

Surrounding streets: Prospect St., Tremont St., Medford St., Ward St., South St., Porter St., Inwood St., Joy St., Linwood St., Hampshire St., Cambridge St., Norfolk St., Harvard St., Washington St., Allen Dr., Massachusetts Ave., Landsdowne Ave., Albany St., Memorial Dr., Harvard Br., Cambridge Pkw.

Back Bay streets: Back St., Beacon St., Bay State Rd., Kenmore Sq., Newbury St., Commonwealth Ave., Boylston St., Marlborough St., Berkeley St., Clarendon St., Stuart St., Blagden St., Carleton St., Columbus Ave., Lawrence St., Hereford St., Gloucester St., Fairfield St., Exeter St., Dartmouth St., Dalton St., Belvidere St., Huntington Ave., St. Botolph St., Ipswich St., Van Ness St., Peterborough St., Queensberry St., Kilmarnock St., Park Dr., Agassiz Rd., Westland Ave., Burbank St., St. Stephen St., Gainsborough St., Hemenway St., Forsyth St., Forsyth Wy., Forsyth Pk., Huntington Ave., Museum Rd., Louis Prang St., Ruggles St., Parker St., Vancouver St., Palace Rd., Columbus Ave., Tremont St., Kendall St., Lenox St., Camden St., Northampton St., Shawmut Ave., Springfield St., Worcester St., W. Springfield St., Wellington St., Rutland Sq., Concord Sq., W. Newton St., W. Rutland Sq., Pembroke St., Warren Ave., W. Canton St., Newland St., Washington St., Concord St.

Brookline Ave., Yawkey Wy., Ness St., Boylston St., Ipswich St.

0 — 1200 feet
0 — 400 meters

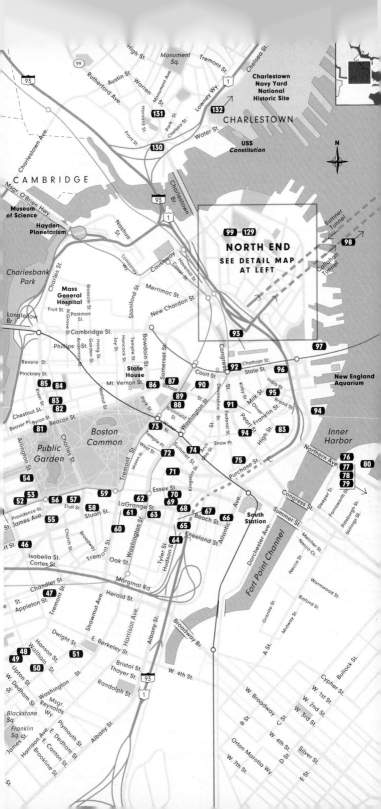

Listed by Site Number

1 Sports Depot
2 Café Brazil
3 Grasshopper
4 Village Fish
5 Five Seasons
6 Zaftigs
7 Elephant Walk
8 Bombay Bistro
9 Taverna de Haro
10 Café St Petersburg
11 Ginza
12 Matt Murphy's
13 El Oriental de Cuba
14 Jake's Boss BBQ
15 Bob the Chef
16 Mike's City Diner
17 House of Siam
18 Jae's Cafe
19 Claremont Café
20 Bangkok Cuisine
21 Dixie Kitchen
22 Clio
23 L'Espalier
24 Casa Romero
25 Sonsie
26 Gyuhama
27 Atlantic Fish Co
28 Abe & Louie's
29 Davio's
30 Emporio Armani Express
31 Morton's of Chicago
32 Stephanie's on Newbury
33 Du Barry
34 Papa Razzi
35 Top of the Hub
36 Brasserie Jo
37 Ambrosia
38 Baja Mexican Cantina
39 Turner Fisheries
40 Small Planet
41 Café Budapest
42 Bertucci's
42 Hard Rock Cafe
43 Skipjack's
44 Café Louis
45 Cottonwood Cafe
46 Grill 23
47 Icarus

48 Truc
49 Hamersley's Bistro
50 On the Park
51 Franklin Café
52 Parish Café
53 Rattlesnake Bar
54 Ritz-Carlton Dining Room
55 Legal Sea Foods
56 Biba
57 Aujourd'hui
57 Bristol Lounge
58 Brew Moon
59 Mercury Bar
60 Montien
61 Jacob Wirth
62 Penang
63 Pho Pasteur
64 Golden Palace
65 New Shanghai
66 Les Zygomates
67 Ho Yuen Ting
68 Imperial Seafood
69 Chau Chow
69 Grand Chau Chow
70 Chau Chow City
71 Café Suisse
72 Fajitas & 'Ritas
73 Locke-Ober Cafe
74 Dakota's
75 Radius
76 The Barking Crab
77 Anthonys Pier 4
78 Jimmy's Harborside
79 Aura
80 No Name
81 Library Grill at Hampshire House
81 Bull & Finch Pub (Cheers)
82 Figs
83 Ristorante Toscano
84 Lala Rokh
85 No 9 Park
85 Hungry i
86 Black Goose
87 The Federalist
88 Café Marliave
89 Parker's
90 Maison Robert
91 Cafe Fleuri

91 Julien
92 Bay Tower Room
93 Marketplace Café
93 Durgin Park
93 Zuma's Tex-Mex Café
94 Country Life
94 Rowes Wharf
95 Nara
95 Sakurabana
96 Tatsukichi
97 Chart House
98 Sablone's
99 Seasons
100 Union Oyster House
101 Joseph's On High
102 Boston Sail Loft
103 Piccolo Nido
104 Florence's
105 Mamma Maria
106 Five North Square
107 Artu
108 La Summa
109 Davide
110 Ristorante Lucia
111 Cantina Italiana
112 Florentine Café
113 Giacomo's
114 G'Vanni's
115 Pomodoro
116 Caffe Vittoria
117 Daily Catch
118 Caffe Paradiso
118 Trattoria a Scalinatella
119 Villa Francesca
120 Mother Anna's
121 Saraceno
122 L'Osteria
123 Nicole
124 Pat's Pushcart
125 Marcuccio's
126 Terramia
127 Massimino's
128 Filippo
129 Dom's
130 Olives
131 Figs
132 Rita's Place

Listed Alphabetically

Abe & Louie's, 28. 793 Boylston St
☎ 536-6300. American. $$$$

Ambrosia, 37. 116 Huntington Ave
☎ 247-2400. Eclectic. $$$$

Anthonys Pier 4, 77. 140 Northern Ave
☎ 423-6363. Seafood. $$$$

Artu, 107. 6 Prince St
☎ 742-4336. Italian. $$

Atlantic Fish Company, 27. 761
Boylston St ☎ 267-4000. Seafood. $$

Aujourd'hui, 57.
Four Seasons Hotel, 200 Boylston St
☎ 351-2071. Continental. $$$$

Aura, 79. Seaport Hotel, 1 Seaport La
☎ 385-4300. Contemporary. $$$$

Baja Mexican Cantina, 38.
111 Dartmouth St ☎ 262-7575.
Mexican. $$

Bangkok Cuisine, 20. 177A Mass Ave
☎ 262-5377. Thai. $$

The Barking Crab, 76. 88 Sleeper St
☎ 426-2722. Seafood. $$

Bay Tower Room, 92. 60 State St
☎ 723-1666. American. $$$$

Bertucci's, 42. 39 Stanhope St
☎ 247-6161. Pizza. $

Biba, 56. 272 Boylston St
☎ 426-7878. Eclectic. $$$$

Black Goose, 86. 21 Beacon St
☎ 720-4500. Italian. $$

Bob the Chef, 15. 604 Columbus Ave
☎ 536-6204. Southern/Cajun. $$

Bombay Bistro, 8. 1353 Beacon St
☎ 734-2879. Indian. $$

Boston Sail Loft, 102. 80 Atlantic Ave
☎ 227-7280. Seafood. $$

Brasserie Jo, 36. 120 Huntington Ave
☎ 425-3240. French. $$$

Brew Moon, 58. 115 Stuart St
☎ 742-2739. Microbrewery. $$

Bristol Lounge, 57. Four Seasons
Hotel, 200 Boylston St ☎ 351-2053.
American. $$$

Bull & Finch Pub (Cheers), 81.
Hampshire House, 84 Beacon St
☎ 227-9605. Pub. $$

Café Brazil, 2. 421 Cambridge St,
Allston ☎ 789-5980. Brazilian. $

Café Budapest, 41. Copley Hotel,
90 Exeter St ☎ 266-1979.
Continental. $$$$

Café Fleuri, 91. Hotel Meridien,
250 Franklin St ☎ 451-1900.
French. $$$

Café Louis, 44. 234 Berkeley St
☎ 266-4680. Italian. $$$$

Café Marliave, 88. 10 Bosworth St
☎ 423-6340. Italian. $$

Café St Petersburg, 10. 236
Washington St, Brookline Village
☎ 566-3474. Russian. $$

Café Suisse, 71. Swissôtel,
1 Ave de Lafayette ☎ 451-2600.
Continental. $$

Caffe Paradiso, 118. 225 Hanover St
☎ 742-1768. Italian/Dessert. $

Caffe Vittoria, 116. 294 Hanover St
☎ 227-7606. Italian. $

Cantina Italiana, 111. 346 Hanover St
☎ 723-4577. Italian. $$

Casa Romero, 24. 30 Gloucester St
☎ 536-4341. Mexican. $$

Chart House, 97. 60 Long Wharf
☎ 227-1576. Seafood. $$$

Chau Chow, 69. 52 Beach St
☎ 292-5166. Cantonese. $

Chau Chow City, 70. 83 Essex St
☎ 338-8158. Chinese. $$

Claremont Café, 19. 535 Columbus
Ave ☎ 247-9001. Mediterranean. $$

Clio, 22. 370 Commonwealth Ave
☎ 536-7200. Eclectic/American. $$$$

Country Life, 94. 200 High St
☎ 951-2534. Vegetarian. $

Cottonwood Cafe, 45. 222 Berkeley St
☎ 247-2225. Southwestern. $$$

Daily Catch, 117. 323 Hanover St
☎ 523-8567. Seafood. $$

Dakota's, 74. 34 Summer St
☎ 737-1777. Steak. $$$

Davide, 109. 326 Commercial Ave
☎ 227-5745. Italian. $$$$

Davio's, 29. 269 Newbury St
☎ 262-4810. Italian. $$$

Dixie Kitchen, 21. 182 Mass Ave
☎ 536-3068. Southern/Cajun. $

Dom's, 129. 10 Bartlett Place
☎ 367-8979. Italian. $$$

Du Barry, 33. 159 Newbury St
☎ 262-2445. French. $$$

Durgin Park, 93. 340 Quincy Mkt
☎ 227-2038. American. $$$

$$$$ = *over $35* $$$ = *$25–$35* $$ = *$15–$25* $ = *under $15*
Based on cost per person, excluding drinks, service, and 5% sales tax.

El Oriental de Cuba, 13. 416 Center St ☎ 524-6464. Caribbean. $$

Elephant Walk, 7. 900 Beacon St ☎ 247-1500. French/Asian. $$$

Emporio Armani Express, 30. 214 Newbury St ☎ 437-0909. Italian. $$$$

Fajitas & 'Ritas, 72. 25 West St ☎ 426-1222. Tex-Mex. $

The Federalist, 87. 15 Beacon St ☎ 670-2515. Contemporary. $$$$

Figs, 82. 42 Charles St ☎ 742-3447. Pizza/Pasta. $

Figs, 131. 67 Main St, Charlestown ☎ 242-2229. Pizza/Pasta. $

Filippo, 128. 283 Causeway St ☎ 742-4143. Italian. $$

Five North Square, 106. 5 North Sq ☎ 720-1050. Italian. $$

Five Seasons, 5. 1634 Beacon St ☎ 731-2500. Macrobiotic. $$$

Florence's, 104. 190 North St ☎ 523-4480. Italian. $$

Florentine Café, 112. 333 Hanover St ☎ 227-1777. Italian. $$$

Franklin Café, 51. 278 Shawmut St ☎ 350-0010. Contemporary. $$

Giacomo's, 113. 355 Hanover St ☎ 523-9026. Italian. $$

Ginza, 11. 1002 Beacon St ☎ 566-3474. Japanese. $$$

Golden Palace, 64. 14 Tyler St ☎ 423-4565. Chinese. $$

Grand Chau Chow, 69. 45 Beach St ☎ 426-6266. Chinese. $

Grasshopper, 3. 1 N Beacon St, Allston ☎ 254-8883. Chinese/Vietnamese-Vegan. $$

Grill 23, 46. 161 Berkeley St ☎ 542-2255. Steak. $$$$

G'Vanni's, 114. 2 Prince St ☎ 523-0107. Italian. $$

Gyuhama, 26. 827 Boylston St ☎ 437-0188. Japanese. $$$

Hamersley's Bistro, 49. 553 Tremont St ☎ 423-2700. Eclectic/French. $$$$

Hard Rock Cafe, 42. 131 Clarendon St ☎ 424-7625. American. $$

Ho Yuen Ting, 67. 13A Hudson St ☎ 426-2316. Chinese/Seafood. $$

House of Siam, 17. 542 Columbus Ave ☎ 267-1755. Thai. $

Hungry i, 85. 71½ Charles St ☎ 227-3524. American. $$$

Icarus, 47. 3 Appleton St ☎ 426-1790. American. $$$$

Imperial Seafood, 68. 70 Beach St ☎ 426-8439. Chinese/Dim Sum. $$

Jacob Wirth, 61. 31 Stuart St ☎ 338-8586. German. $$

Jae's Cafe, 18. 520 Columbus Ave ☎ 421-9405. Korean. $$

Jake's Boss BBQ, 14. 3924 Washington St ☎ 983-3701. Soul Food. $$

Jimmy's Harborside, 78. 242 Northern Ave ☎ 423-1000. Seafood. $$$

Joseph's On High, 101. 101 Atlantic Ave ☎ 523-4000. Seafood. $$$

Julien, 91. Hotel Meridien, 250 Franklin St ☎ 451-1900. French. $$$$

La Summa, 108. 30 Fleet St ☎ 523-9503. Italian. $$

Lala Rokh, 84. 97 Mount Vernon St ☎ 720-5511. Persian. $$$

Legal Sea Foods, 55. Park Plaza ☎ 426-4444. Seafood. $$$

L'Espalier, 23. 30 Gloucester St ☎ 262-3023. French. $$$$

Les Zygomates, 66. 129 South St ☎ 542-5108. French Bistro. $$$

Library Grill at Hampshire House, 81. 84 Beacon St ☎ 227-9600. American. $$$

Locke-Ober Cafe, 73. 3 Winter Pl ☎ 542-1340. American. $$$$

L'Osteria, 122. 104 Salem St ☎ 723-7847. Italian. $$

Maison Robert, 90. 45 School St ☎ 227-3370. French. $$$

Mamma Maria, 105. 3 North Sq ☎ 523-0077. Italian. $$$$

Marcuccio's, 125. 125 Salem St ☎ 723-1807. Italian. $$$

Marketplace Café, 93. Quincy Market ☎ 227-1272. American. $$

Massimino's, 127. 207 Endicott St ☎ 523-5959. Italian. $$

Matt Murphy's Pub, 12. 14 Harvard St ☎ 232-0188. Irish. $$

Mercury Bar, 55. 116 Boylston St ☎ 482-7799. Eclectic. $$$

Mike's City Diner, 16. 1714 Washington St ☎ 267-9393. American. $

Listed Alphabetically (cont.)

Montien, 60. 63 Stuart St
☎ 338-5600. Thai. $$

Morton's of Chicago, 31. 1 Exeter Pl
☎ 266-5858. Steak. $$$$

Mother Anna's, 120. 211 Hanover St
☎ 523-8496. Italian. $$

Nara, 95. 85 Wendell St
☎ 338-5395. Japanese/Korean. $$

New Shanghai, 65. 21 Hudson St
☎ 338-6688. Chinese. $$

Nicole, 123. 54 Salem St
☎ 742-6999. Italian. $$

No Name, 80. 15½ Fish Pier, off
Northern Ave ☎ 338-7539.
Seafood. $$

No 9 Park, 85. 9 Park St
☎ 742-9991. Contemporary. $$$$

Olives, 130. 10 City Sq,
Charlestown ☎ 242-1999.
Italian/Mediterranean. $$$

On the Park, 50. 315 Shawmut Ave
☎ 426-0862. American. $$

Papa Razzi, 34. 271 Dartmouth St
☎ 536-9200. Italian/Med. $$$

Parish Café, 52. 361 Boylston St
☎ 247-4777. American. $

Parker's, 89. Omni Parker Hse, 60
School St ☎ 227-8600. American. $$$$

Pat's Pushcart, 124. 61 Endicott St
☎ 523-9616. Italian. $$

Penang, 62. 685 Washington St
☎ 451-6372. Malaysian. $$$

Pho Pasteur, 63. 8 Kneeland St
☎ 451-0247. Vietnamese. $

Piccolo Nido, 103. 257 North St
☎ 742-4272. Italian. $$

Pomodoro, 115. 319 Hanover St
☎ 367-4348. Italian. $$

Radius, 75. 8 High St
☎ 426-1234. Eclectic/French. $$$$

Rattlesnake Bar, 53. 384 Boylston St
☎ 859-8555. American. $

Ristorante Lucia, 110. 415 Hanover St
☎ 367-2353. Italian. $$$

Ristorante Toscano, 83. 41 Charles St
☎ 723-4090. Italian. $$$

Rita's Place, 132. 88 Winnisimmet St,
Chelsea ☎ 884-9010. Italian. $$$

Ritz-Carlton, 54. 15 Arlington St
☎ 536-5700. American. $$$

Rowes Wharf Restaurant, 94.
Boston Harbor Hotel, Atlantic
Ave ☎ 439-3995. Seafood.
$$$$

Sablone's, 98. 107A Porter St
☎ 567-8140. Italian. $$$

Sakurabana, 95. 57 Broad St
☎ 542-4311. Japanese. $$

Saraceno, 121. 286 Hanover St
☎ 227-5888. Italian. $$$

Seasons, 99. Bostonian Hotel, 9
Blackstone St ☎ 523-4119.
Continental. $$$$

Skipjack's, 43. 199 Clarendon St
☎ 536-3500. Seafood. $$$

Small Planet, 40. 565 Boylston St
☎ 536-4477. International. $

Sonsie, 25. 327 Newbury St
☎ 351-2500. International. $$

Sports Depot, 1. 353 Cambridge St,
Allston ☎ 783-2300. American. $$

Stephanie's on Newbury, 32.
190 Newbury St ☎ 236-0990.
American. $$$

Taberna de Haro, 9. 999 Beacon St
☎ 277-8272. Spanish. $$$

Tatsukichi, 96. 189 State St
☎ 720-2468. Japanese. $$$

Terramia, 126. 98 Salem St
☎ 523-3112. Italian. $$$

Top of the Hub, 35. Prudential Ctr
☎ 536-1775. American. $$$$

Trattoria a Scalinatella, 118. 255
Hanover St ☎ 742-8240. Italian. $$$

Trident Booksellers & Café, 19.
338 Newbury St ☎ 267-8688. Café. $

Truc, 48. 560 Tremont St
☎ 338-8070. French. $$$

Turner Fisheries, 39. Westin Hotel,
10 Huntington Ave ☎ 424-7425 $$$

Union Oyster House, 100. 41 Union St
☎ 227-2750. Seafood/Raw Bar. $$

Villa Francesca, 119. 150 Richmond St
☎ 367-2948. Italian. $$

Village Fish, 4. 22 Harvard St,
Brookline ☎ 566-3474. Seafood. $$

Zaftigs, 6. 335 Harvard St
☎ 975-0075. Delicatessen. $$

Zuma's Tex-Mex Cafe, 93. Quincy
Mkt ☎ 367-9114. Tex-Mex. $$$

$$$$ = *over $35* $$$ = *$25–$35* $$ = *$15–$25* $ = *under $15*
Based on cost per person, excluding drinks, service, and 5% sales tax.

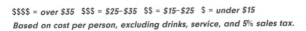

MAP **47** Restaurants/Cambridge & Somerville

Richdale Ave.
Hubbard Ave.
Richardson Ave.
Raymond St.
Mt. Pleasant St.
Mt. Vincent St.
Upland Rd.
Washington Ave.
Arlington St.
Porter Sq.
Elm St.
Summer St.
Craigie Ter.
Porter St.
Moseland
Somerville Ave.
Lowell St.
Craigie St.
Belmont St.

1 **2** **3**
4
5
2A

St. Peters Field
Sherman St.
Newell St.
Winslow Ave.
Huron Ave.
Donnell St.
Walden St.

Hillside Ave.
Hillside
Avon St.
Avon Hill
Bowdoin St.
Martin St.

Frost St.
Forest St.
Prentiss St.
Garfield St.
Eustis St.
Sacramento St.
Harris St.
Carver St.
Beacon St.
Harrison St.

6
7
8

Linnaean St.
Walker St.
Shepard St.
Walker St.
Chauncy St.
Follen St.

Madison St.
Bond St.
Garden St.
Concord Ave.
Berkeley St.

Radcliffe College

Wendell St.
Mellen St.
Everett St.
Hammond
Museum St.
Francis Ave.
Bryant St.
Irving St.
Holden
Kirkland St.
Trowbridge St.

9
10

Highland St.
Brewster St.
Sparks St.
Brattle St.
Foster St.
Craigie
Willard St.
Brattle St.
Hawthorn St.
Mt. Auburn St.
Pk.

Harvard University

Oxford St.

Cambridge St.

3
2

Eliot Br.

Charles River

Memorial Dr.

Waterhouse St.
Cambridge Common
Radcliffe Yard
Hilliard St.
Appian Wy.
Church St.
Peabody Sq.
Harvard Yard

Quincy St.
Prescott St.
Broadway
Ellery St.
Chatham
Trowbridge St.
Ware St.
Ellery St.
Harvard

11
12
13
14
15
16
17
18
19
20
21
22 **23**
24
25
26
27

Harvard Sq.

Hilliard St.
Winthrop St.
JFK St.
Dunster St.
Holyoke St.
Plympton St.
Mt. Auburn St.
Bow St.
De Wolfe St.
Mill St.
Grant St.
Banks St.
Green St.
Massachusetts Ave.
Putnam
Magee St.
Flagg St. Plgd.
Hingham St.
Franklin St.
Kinnaird St.
Howard St.
Bay St.
Jay St.
Pleasant St.
Fairmont St.

Anderson Br.

ALLSTON

Soldiers Field Rd.
N. Harvard St.
Gordan Dr.
Western Ave. Br.
Western Ave.
Rotterdam St.
Hague St.
Blackstone St.

Hoyt Field

3
2

N

0 ——— 1500 feet
0 ——— 500 meters

Franklin St. Kingsley St.

River St. Br.
River St.

29 **28**

Listed by Site Number

1	Redbones	9	Lucky Garden	17	Iruna
2	Gargoyles on the Sq	10	Full Moon	18	Bertucci's
3	Elephant Walk	11	Algiers Café	18	Casa Mexico
4	Porterhouse Café	12	Casablanca	19	John Harvard's
5	Cottonwood Café	13	Harvest	20	Tealuxe
6	Changsho	14	Grendel's Den	21	Border Cafe
7	Forest Café	15	Rialto	22	Grafton St Pub & Grill
8	Chez Henri	16	Tanjore	23	Up Stairs at the Pudding

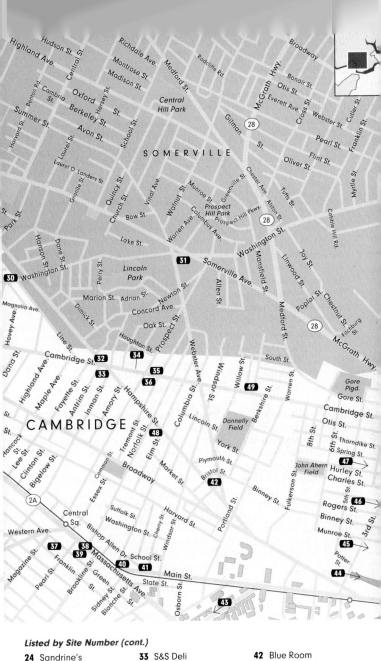

Listed by Site Number (cont.)

24 Sandrine's	**33** S&S Deli	**42** Blue Room
25 Bartley's	**34** East Coast Grill	**43** Spinnaker Italia
26 Cafe Sushi	**35** Magnolia's	**44** Poppa & Goose
27 Roka	**36** Casa Portugal	**45** Salamander
28 Dionysos	**37** India Pavilion	**46** Helmand
29 Bisuteki	**38** Shalimar of India	**47** Boca Grande
30 Dali	**39** Green St Grill	**48** Daddy O's
31 eat	**40** Rhythm & Spice	**49** Sunset Café
32 Druid	**41** La Groceria	

Listed Alphabetically

Algiers Café, 11. Brattle Thtre, ☎ 492-1557. Middle Eastern. $

Bartley's Burger Cottage, 25. 1246 Mass Ave ☎ 354-6559. Burgers. $

Bertucci's, 18. 21 Brattle St ☎ 864-4748. Pizza. $

Bisuteki, 29. 777 Memorial Drive ☎ 492-7777. Japanese/Steak. $$

Blue Room, 42. 1 Kendall Square ☎ 494-9034. Eclectic. $$$

Boca Grande, 47. 149 First St ☎ 354-5550. Mexican. $

The Border Cafe, 21. 32 Church St ☎ 864-6100. Mexican/Cajun. $$

Cafe Sushi, 26. 1105 Mass Ave ☎ 492-0434. Japanese. $$

Casa Mexico, 18. 75 Winthrop St ☎ 491-4552. Mexican. $$

Casa Portugal, 36. 1200 Cambridge St ☎ 491-8880. Portuguese. $$

Casablanca, 12. 40 Brattle St ☎ 876-0999. Seafood/Pasta. $$

Changsho, 6. 1712 Mass Ave ☎ 547-6565. Mandarin/Szechuan. $$

Chez Henri, 8. 1 Shepard St ☎ 354-8980. French. $$$

Cottonwood Café, 5. 1815 Mass Ave ☎ 661-7440. Southwestern. $$

Daddy O's Bohemian Cafe, 48. 134 Hampshire St ☎ 354-8371. Eclectic. $

Dali, 30. 415 Washington St, Som ☎ 661-3254. Spanish. $$$

Dionysos, 28. 777 Memorial Dr ☎ 661-6800. Greek. $$

Druid, 32. 1357 Cambridge St ☎ 497-0965. Irish. $

East Coast Grill, 34. 1271 Cambridge St ☎ 491-6568. BBQ/Seafood. $$$

eat, 31. 253 Washington St ☎ 776-2889. New American. $$$

Elephant Walk, 3. 2067 Mass Ave ☎ 492-6900. French/Asian. $$$

Forest Café, 7. 1682 Mass Ave ☎ 661-7810. Mexican. $$

Full Moon, 10. 344 Huron Ave ☎ 354-6699. New American. $$

Gargoyles on the Square, 2. 215 Elm St ☎ 776-5300. New American. $$$

Grafton St Pub & Grill, 22. 1280 Mass Ave ☎ 497-0400. American. $$

Green St Grill, 39. 280 Green St ☎ 876-1655. Caribbean. $$

Grendel's Den, 14. 89 Winthrop St ☎ 491-1160. American. $$

Harvest, 13. 44 Brattle St ☎ 868-2255. American. $$$

The Helmand, 46. 143 First St ☎ 492-4646. Afghan. $$$

India Pavilion, 37. 17 Central Sq ☎ 547-7463. Indian. $$

Iruna, 17. 56 JFK St ☎ 868-5633. Spanish. $$

John Harvard's Brew House, 19. 33 Dunster St ☎ 868-3585. American. $$

La Groceria, 41. 853 Main St ☎ 497-4214. Italian. $$

Lucky Garden, 9. 282 Concord Ave ☎ 354-9514. Chinese. $

Magnolia's, 35. 1193 Cambridge St ☎ 576-1971. Cajun. $$

Poppa & Goose, 44. 69 First St ☎ 497-6772. Asian. $$

Porterhouse Café, 4. 2046 Mass Ave ☎ 354-9793. BBQ. $$

Redbones, 1. 55 Chester St, Som ☎ 225-2121. BBQ/Southern $$

Rhythm & Spice, 40. 315 Mass Ave ☎ 497-0977. Caribbean. $$

Rialto, 15. Charles Hotel, Harvard Sq ☎ 661-5050. American. $$$$

Roka, 27. 1001 Mass Ave ☎ 661-0344. Japanese. $$

S&S Deli, 33. 1334 Cambridge St ☎ 354-0777. Deli. $

Salamander, 45. 1 Athenaeum St ☎ 225-2121. New American. $$$$

Sandrine's, 24. 8 Holyoke St ☎ 497-5300. Alsatian. $$$$

Shalimar of India, 38. 546 Mass Ave ☎ 547-9280. Indian. $$

Spinnaker Italia, 43. Hyatt Regency Hotel ☎ 492-1234. Italian. $$$

Sunset Café, 48. 851 Cambridge St ☎ 547-2938. Portuguese. $$

Tanjore, 16. 18 Eliot St ☎ 868-1900. Indian. $$

Tealuxe, 9. Zero Brattle St ☎ 441-0077. Tearoom. $

Up Stairs at the Pudding, 21. 10 Holyoke St ☎ 864-1933. Cont. $$$

$$$$ = over $35 $$$ = $25-$35 $$ = $15-$25 $ = under $15
Based on cost per person, excluding drinks, service, and 5% sales tax.

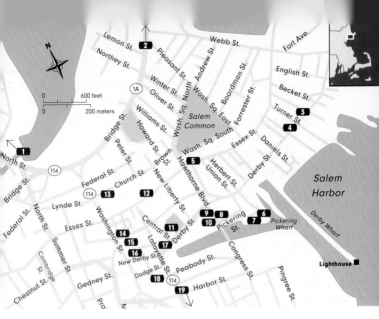

Listed by Site Number

1	Kiki's Chinese Food	8	Asahi	14	Café Graziani
2	Stromberg's	9	Grapevine	15	Lobster Shanty
3	Derby Fish & Lobster	10	Red Raven's Love Noodle	16	Olde Village Beanery
4	In a Pig's Eye	11	Roosevelt's	17	Salem Beer Works
5	Nathaniel's	12	Thai Place	18	Dodge St Grill
6	Victoria Station	13	Lyceum	19	Salem Diner
7	Chase House				

Listed Alphabetically

Asahi, 8. 21 Congress St
☎ 978/744-5376. Japanese. $$

Café Graziani, 14. 133 Washington St
☎ 978/741-4282. Italian. $$

Chase House, 7. Pickering Wharf
☎ 978/744-0000. Seafood. $$

Derby Fish & Lobster, 3. 215 Derby St
☎ 978/745-2064. Seafood. $$

Dodge St Grill, 18. 7 Dodge St
☎ 978/745-0139. American. $$

Grapevine, 9. 26 Congress St
☎ 978/745-9335. American/Italian. $$

In a Pig's Eye, 4. 148 Derby St
☎ 978/741-4436. American. $$

Kiki's Chinese Food, 1. 127 Boston St
☎ 978/744-3777. Chinese. $

Lobster Shanty, 15. Salem Mktpl
☎ 978/745-7449. American. $$

Lyceum, 13. 43 Church St
☎ 978/745-7665. Continental. $$

Nathaniel's, 5. Hawthorne Inn Hotel
☎ 978/744-4080. American. $$$

Olde Village Beanery Cafe, 16.
14 New Derby St ☎ 978/740-3070.
American. $

Red Raven's Love Noodle, 10.
75 Congress St ☎ 978/745-8558.
Eclectic. $$

Roosevelt's, 11. 300 Derby St
☎ 978/745-9608. American. $$

Salem Beer Works, 17. 278 Derby St
☎ 978/745-2337. Microbrewery. $$

Salem Diner, 19. 70 Loring Ave
☎ 978/744-9776. American. $

Stromberg's, 2. 2 Bridge St
☎ 978/744-1863. Seafood/Amer. $$

Thai Place, 12. Museum Place Mall
☎ 978/741-8008. Thai. $$

Victoria Station, 6. Pickering Wharf
☎ 978/745-3400. American. $$

$$$$ = over $35 $$$ = $25-$35 $$ = $15-$25 $ = under $15
Based on cost per person, excluding drinks, service, and 5% sales tax.

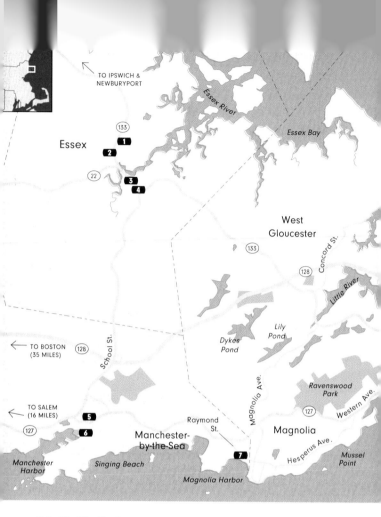

Listed by Site Number

1	Woodman's	4	Tom Shea's	7	Edgewater Café
2	Blue Marlin Grill	5	Seven Central	8	The Rhumb Line
3	JP's Hearthside	6	Harborside Hofbrau	9	White Rainbow

Listed Alphabetically

Blue Marlin Grill, 2.
65 Eastern Ave, Essex
☎ 978/768-7400. American. $

Cameron's, 10. 206 Main St,
Gloucester ☎ 978/281-1331.
American. $$

Edgewater Café, 7. 69 Raymond St,
Manchester-by-the-Sea
☎ 978/526-4668. Mexican. $

Greenery, 15. Dock Sq, Rockport
☎ 978/546-9593. Seafood. $$

The Gull, 14. 75 Essex St, Gloucester
☎ 978/283-6565. Seafood. $$

Halibut Point, 13. 289 Main St,
Gloucester ☎ 978/281-1900.
American. $

Harborside Hofbrau, 6. 37 Beach St,
Manchester-by-the-Sea ☎ 978/526-
7774. German/American. $$

JP's Hearthside, 3. Rt 133,
Essex ☎ 978/768-6003.
Seafood/American. $$

L'Amante, 11. 197 E Main St,
Gloucester ☎ 978/282-4426.
Italian/French. $$

Listed by Site Number (cont.)

10 Cameron's

11 L'Amante

12 Ocean View Inn

13 Halibut Point

14 The Gull

15 Greenery

16 Portside Chowder House

17 My Place by the Sea

Listed Alphabetically (cont.)

My Place by the Sea, 17. Bearskin Neck, Rockport ☎ 978/546-9667. Seafood. $$

Ocean View Inn, 12. 171 Atlantic Rd, Gloucester ☎ 978/283-6200. American. $$$

Portside Chowder House, 16. Doyles Cove Rd, Rockport. ☎ 978/546-7045. American. $

The Rhumb Line, 8. Railroad Ave, Gloucester ☎ 978/283-9732. American. $$$

Seven Central, 5. Rt 127, Manchester-by-the-Sea ☎ 978/526-7494. American. $$$

Tom Shea's, 4. 122 Main St, Essex ☎ 978/768-6931. Seafood/American. $$$

White Rainbow, 9. 65 Main St, Gloucester ☎ 978/281-0017. American. $$$

Woodman's, 1. Rt 133, Essex ☎ 978/768-6451. Seafood. $

$$$$ = over $35 $$$ = $25-$35 $$ = $15-$25 $ = under $15

Based on cost per person, excluding drinks, service, and 5% sales tax.

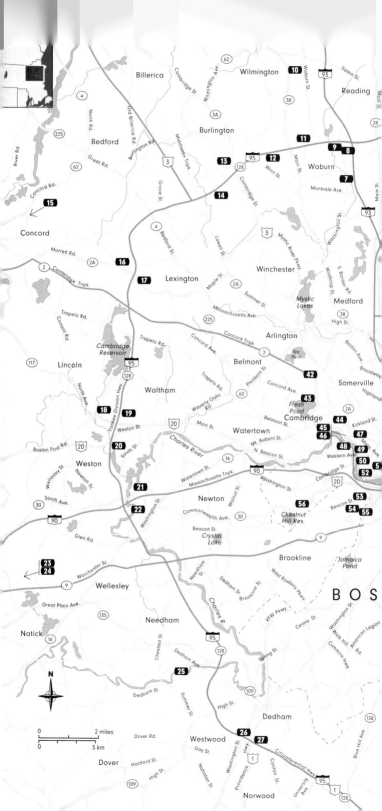

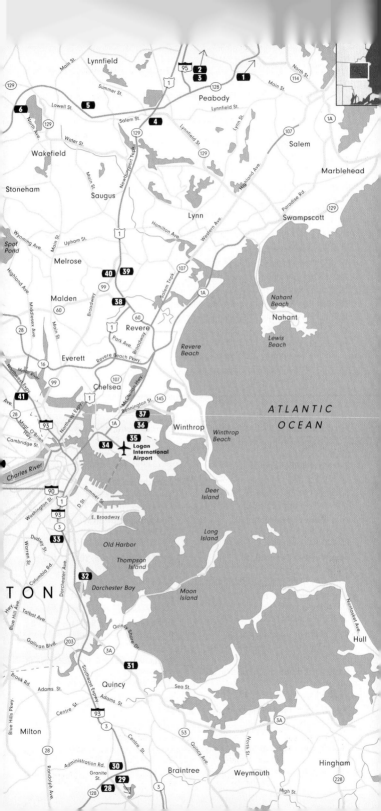

Listed by Site Number

1 Quality Inn
2 Comfort Inn
3 Marriott Peabody
4 Holiday Inn
5 Sheraton Colonial
6 Best Western Lord Wakefield
7 HoJo Woburn
8 Holiday Inn Crowne Plaza
9 Hampton Inn
10 Red Roof Inn
11 Courtyard Marriott
12 Ramada Woburn
13 Marriott Burlington
14 Four Points Barcelo
15 Best Western Conc
16 Sheraton Lexington
17 Battle Green Inn
18 Doubletree Guest Suites Waltham
19 Best Western East

20 Westin Waltham
21 Marriott Newton
22 Holiday Inn Newton
23 Holiday Inn Crowne Plaza
24 Sheraton
25 Inn on the Square
26 Holiday Inn
27 Comfort Inn Dedham
28 Sheraton
29 Motel 6
30 Days Inn Braintree
31 Best Western Adams Inn
32 Susse Chalet Motor Lodges
33 Holiday Inn Express
34 Hyatt Harborside
35 Hilton Logan Airport
36 Airport Ramada
37 Holiday Inn Airport
38 Town Line Inn
39 HoJo Revere

40 Days Inn Saugus
41 Holiday Inn
42 Susse Chalet Inn
43 Best Western Homestead
44 Sheraton Commander
45 Charles Hotel
46 Harvard Sq Hotel
47 Inn at Harvard
48 Doubletree Guest Suites Hotel
49 Harding House
50 HoJo Cambridge
51 University Park
52 Hyatt Regency
53 Holiday Inn
54 Bertram Inn
55 Best Western Inn at Children's
56 Best Western Terrace

Listed Alphabetically

Airport Ramada, 36. Logan Airport
☎ 569-9300. 🖷 567-1947. $$$

Battle Green Inn, 17.
1720 Mass Ave, Lexington
☎ 781/862-6100. 🖷 781/861-9485. $

Bertram Inn, 54. 92 Sewall Ave,
Brookline ☎ 566-2234. 🖷 277-1887. $$$

Best Western Adams Inn, 31.
29 Hancock St, Quincy
☎ 328-1500. 🖷 328-3067. $

Best Western Concord, 15.
740 Elm St, Concord
☎ 978/369-6100. 🖷 978/371-1656. $

Best Western East, 19.
477 Totten Pd Rd, Waltham
☎ 781/890-7800. 🖷 781/890-4937. $

Best Western Homestead, 43.
220 Alewife Brook Pkwy, Cambridge
☎ 491-1890. 🖷 491-4932. $$

Best Western Inn at Children's, 55.
342 Longwood Ave
☎ 731-4700. 🖷 731-6273. $$

Best Western Lord Wakefield, 6.
595 North Ave, Wakefield
☎ 781/245-6100. 🖷 781/245-2904. $

Best Western Terrace Inn, 56. 1650
Commonwealth Ave, Brighton
☎ 566-6260. 🖷 731-3543. $

Charles Hotel, 45. 1 Bennett Sq, Cam
☎ 864-1200. 🖷 864-5715. $$$$

Comfort Inn, 2. 50 Dayton St, Danvers
☎ 978/777-1700. 🖷 978/777-4647. $

Comfort Inn Dedham, 27.
235 Elm St, Dedham
☎ 781/326-6700. 🖷 781/326-9264. $

Courtyard Marriott Woburn, 11.
240 Mishawum Rd, Woburn
☎ 781/932-3200. 🖷 781/935-6163. $$

Days Inn Braintree, 30. 190 Wood
Rd, Braintree ☎ 781/848-1260.
🖷 781/848-9799. $

Days Inn Saugus, 40. Rt 1, Saugus
☎ 781/233-1800. 🖷 781/233-1814. $

Doubletree Guest Suites Hotel, 48.
400 Soldiers Field Rd
☎ 783-0090. 🖷 783-0897. $$$

Doubletree Guest Suites Waltham, 18.
550 Winter St, Waltham
☎ 781/890-6767. 🖷 781/890-8197. $$$

Four Points Barcelo, 14.
Wheeler Rd, Burlington
☎ 781/272-8800. 🖷 781/221-4605. $$

Hampton Inn Woburn, 9.
315 Mishawum Rd, Woburn
☎ 781/935-7666. 🖷 781/933-6899. $

Harding House, 49.
288 Harvard St, Cambridge
☎ 876-2888. 📠 497-0953. $$

Harvard Sq Hotel, 46.
110 Mt Auburn St, Cambridge
☎ 864-5200. 📠 864-2409. $$$

Hilton Logan Airport, 35.
85 Terminal Rd, Logan Airport
☎ 568-6700. 📠 568-6800. $$$

Holiday Inn, 4. Rt I, Peabody
☎ 978/535-4600. 📠 978/535-8238. $$

Holiday Inn, 26. Rts I & 128, Dedham
☎ 781/329-1000. 📠 781/329-0903. $$

Holiday Inn, 41.
30 Washington St, Somerville
☎ 628-1000. 📠 628-0143. $$$

Holiday Inn, 53. 1200 Beacon St,
Brookline ☎ 277-1200. 📠 734-6991. $$

Holiday Inn Airport, 37. Rt IA,
E Boston ☎ 569-5250. 📠 569-5159. $$$

Holiday Inn Crowne Plaza, 8.
2 Forbes Rd, Woburn ☎ 781/932-0999.
📠 781/932-0903. $$$

Holiday Inn Crowne Plaza, 23. 1360
Worcester Rd, Natick ☎ 508/653-8800.
📠 508/653-1708. $$$

Holiday Inn Express, 33.
69 Boston St, Dorchester
☎ 288-3030. 📠 265-6543. $

Holiday Inn Newton, 22.
399 Grove St, Newton
☎ 969-5300. 📠 965-4280. $$

Howard Johnson's Cambridge, 50.
777 Memorial Dr, Cambridge
☎ 492-7777. 📠 492-6038. $$$

Howard Johnson's Revere, 39.
407 Squire Rd, Revere
☎ 781/284-7200. 📠 781/289-3176. $

Howard Johnson's Woburn, 7.
Montvale Ave, Woburn
☎ 781/935-8160. 📠 781/932-9623. $

Hyatt Harborside, 34. 101 Harborside
Dr, Logan Airport ☎ 568-1234.
📠 567-8856. $$$$

Hyatt Regency, 52.
575 Memorial Dr, Cambridge
☎ 492-1234. 📠 491-6906. $$$$

Inn at Harvard, 47. 1201 Mass Ave,
Cam ☎ 491-2222. 📠 491-6520. $$$$

Inn on the Square, 25.
576 Washington St, Wellesley
☎ 781/235-0180. 📠 781/235-5263. $$

Marriott Burlington, 13.
Rts 128 & 3A, Burlington
☎ 781/229-6565. 📠 781/630-3523.
$$$

Marriott Newton, 21.
Commonwealth Ave, Newton
☎ 969-1000. 📠 527-6914. $$$

Marriott Peabody, 3. Rt 128,
Peabody ☎ 978/977-9700.
📠 978/977-0297. $$

Motel 6, 29. 125 Union St, Braintree
☎ 781/848-7890. 📠 781/843-1929. $

Quality Inn, 1. Rt 128, Danvers
☎ 978/774-6800. 📠 978/774-6502. $$$

Ramada Woburn, 12. Rts 38 & 128,
Woburn ☎ 781/935-8760.
📠 781/938-1790. $$

Red Roof Inn Woburn, 10.
19 Commerce Way, Woburn
☎ 781/935-7110. 📠 781/932-0657. $

Sheraton, 28. 37 Forbes St, Braintree
☎ 781/848-0600. 📠 781/843-9492. $$$

Sheraton, 24. 1657 Worcester Rd,
Framingham ☎ 508/879-7200.
📠 508/875-7593. $$$

Sheraton Colonial, 5. Rt 128,
Wakefield ☎ 781/245-9300.
📠 781/245-0842. $$$

Sheraton Commander, 44.
16 Garden St, Cambridge
☎ 547-4800. 📠 868-8322. $$$

Sheraton Lexington, 16. 727 Marrett
Rd, Lexington ☎ 781/862-8700.
📠 781/863-0404. $$$

Susse Chalet Inn, 42.
211 Concord Tnpk, Cambridge
☎ 661-7800. 📠 868-8153. $

Susse Chalet Motor Lodges, 32.
800 & 900 Morrissey Blvd
☎ 287-9100, 287-9200.
📠 265-9287, 282-2365. $

Town Line Inn, 38. Rt I, Malden
☎ 781/324-7400. 📠 781/397-8501. $$

University Park Hotel at MIT, 51.
20 Sidney St ☎ 577-0200.
📠 494-8366. $$$

Westin Waltham, 20. 70 Third Ave,
Waltham ☎ 781/290-5600.
📠 781/290-5636. $$$$

$$$$ = *over $190* $$$ = *$130-$190* $$ = *$100-$130* $ = *under $100*
Prices are for a standard double room, excluding 9.7% room tax.

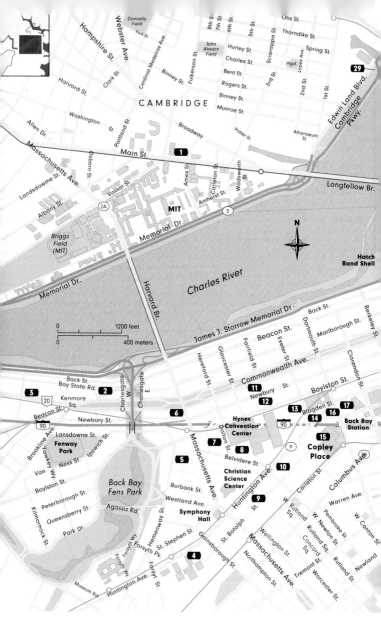

Listed by Site Number

1 Cambridge Center Marriott

2 Gryphon House

3 Howard Johnson's Kenmore Square

4 Greater Boston YMCA

5 Boston International Hostel

6 Eliot Hotel

7 Back Bay Hilton

8 Sheraton

9 Midtown Hotel

10 The Colonnade

11 Newbury Guest House

12 Beacon Inns

13 Lenox Hotel

14 Copley Square

15 Marriott Copley Place

16 Westin Hotel

MAP 51

CHARLESTOWN

Listed by Site Number (cont.)

17 Fairmont Copley Plaza	**23** Four Seasons	**30** Regal Bostonian
18 Chandler Inn Hotel	**24** Swissôtel	**31** Marriott Long Wharf
19 Berkeley Residence YWCA	**25** Omni Parker House	**32** Harborside Inn
20 Tremont House	**26** Fifteen Beacon	**33** Wyndham Boston
21 Boston Park Plaza	**27** Holiday Inn-Gov't Ctr	**34** Le Meridien
22 Ritz-Carlton	**28** John Jeffries House	**35** Boston Harbor Hotel
	29 Royal Sonesta	**36** Seaport Hotel

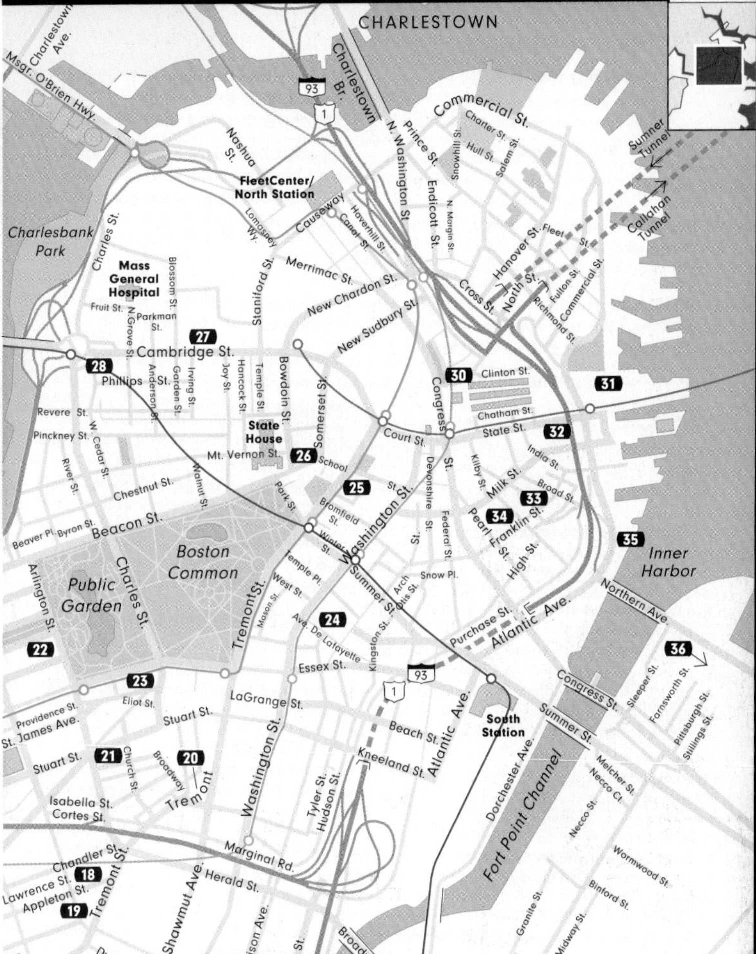

Listed Alphabetically

Back Bay Hilton, 7.
40 Dalton St
☎ 236-1100. ☏ 867-6139. $$$

Beacon Inns & Guesthouses, 12.
248 Newbury St
☎ 266-7142. ☏ 266-7276. $

**Berkeley Residence YWCA
(Women), 19.** 40 Berkeley St
☎ 375-2524. ☏ 375-2525. $

Boston Harbor Hotel, 35.
70 Rowes Wharf
☎ 439-7000. ☏ 345-6799. $$$$

Boston International Hostel, 5.
12 Hemenway St
☎ 536-9455. ☏ 424-6558. $

**Boston Park Plaza Hotel &
Towers, 21.** 64 Arlington St
☎ 426-2000. ☏ 423-1708. $$$$

Cambridge Center Marriott, 1.
2 Cambridge Center
☎ 494-6600 ☏ 494-0036. $$$

Chandler Inn Hotel, 18.
26 Chandler St
☎ 482-3450. ☏ 542-3428. $

The Colonnade, 10.
120 Huntington Ave
☎ 424-7000. ☏ 424-1717. $$$

Copley Square, 14.
47 Huntington Ave
☎ 536-9000. ☏ 267-3547. $$

Eliot Hotel, 6.
370 Commonwealth Ave
☎ 267-1607. ☏ 536-9114. $$

Fairmont Copley Plaza, 17.
Copley Sq ☎ 267-5300. ☏ 267-7668.
$$$$

Fifteen Beacon, 26. 15 Beacon St
☎ 670-1500. ☏ 670-2525. $$$$

Four Seasons, 23. 200 Boylston St
☎ 338-4400. ☏ 423-0154. $$$$

Greater Boston YMCA, 4.
316 Huntington Ave ☎ 536-7800.
☏ 267-4653. $

Gryphon House, 2. 9 Bay State Rd
☎ 375-9003. ☏ 425-0716. $$$

Harborside Inn, 32. 185 State St
☎ 723-7500. ☏ 670-2010. $$$

**Holiday Inn-Government
Center, 27.** 5 Blossom St
☎ 742-7630. ☏ 742-4192. $$

Howard Johnson's Kenmore Sq, 3.
575 Commonwealth Ave
☎ 267-3100. ☏ 424-1045. $$

John Jeffries House, 28.
14 David G. Mugar Way
☎ 367-1866. ☏ 742-0313. $$

Le Meridien, 34. 250 Franklin St
☎ 451-1900. ☏ 423-2844. $$$$

Lenox Hotel, 13. 710 Boylston St
☎ 536-5300. ☏ 236-0351. $$$$

Marriott Copley Place, 15.
110 Huntington Ave
☎ 236-5800. ☏ 236-5885. $$$$

Marriott Long Wharf, 31. 296 State St
☎ 227-0800. ☏ 227-2867. $$$$

Midtown Hotel, 9.
220 Huntington Ave
☎ 262-1000. ☏ 262--8739. $$

Newbury Guest House, 11.
261 Newbury St
☎ 437-7666. ☏ 262-4243. $

Omni Parker House, 25. 60 School St
☎ 227-8600. ☏ 742-5729. $$$

Regal Bostonian, 30.
Faneuil Hall Marketplace
☎ 523-3600. ☏ 523-2454. $$$$

Ritz-Carlton, 22. 15 Arlington St
☎ 536-5700. ☏ 536-1335. $$$$

Royal Sonesta, 29.
5 Cambridge Pkwy
☎ 491-3600. ☏ 661-5956. $$$

Seaport Hotel, 36.   1
Seaport La, World Trade Ctr
☎ 385-4000. ☏ 385-5090. $$$

Sheraton Boston Hotel & Towers, 8.
39 Dalton St
☎ 236-2000. ☏ 236-6095. $$$

Swissôtel, 24. 1 Ave de Lafayette
☎ 451-2600. $$$$

Tremont House, 20. 275 Tremont St
☎ 426-1400. ☏ 338-7881. $$

Westin, 16. 10 Huntington Ave
☎ 262-9600. ☏ 424-7502. $$$$

Wyndham Boston, 33. 89 Broad St
☎ 556-0006. ☏ 556-0053. $$$

$$$$ = *over $190* $$$ = *$130–$190* $$ = *$100–$130* $ = *under $100*
Prices are for a standard double room, excluding 9.7% tax and service charges.

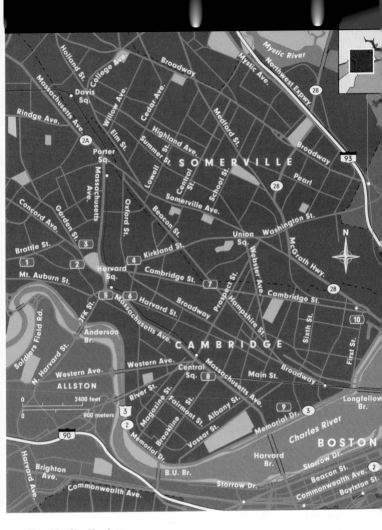

Listed by Site Number

1 New School of Music

2 American Repertory Theatre/Loeb Drama Center

3 Longy Sch of Music

4 Sanders Theater

5 Hasty Pudding Theatre

6 Comedy Studio

7 Back Alley Theatre

8 Dance Complex

9 Kresge Auditorium

10 Cambridge Multicultural Arts Center

Listed Alphabetically

American Rep Theatre/Loeb Drama Center, 2. 64 Brattle St ☎ 547-8300

Back Alley Theatre/ImprovBoston, 7. 1253 Cambridge St ☎ 576-1253

Cambridge Multicultural Arts Center, 10. 41 Second St ☎ 577-1400

Comedy Studio, 6. 1236 Mass Ave ☎ 661-6507

Dance Complex, 8. 536 Mass Ave ☎ 547-9363

Hasty Pudding Theatre/Harvard, 5. 12 Holyoke St ☎ 495-5205

Kresge Auditorium/MIT, 9. 77 Mass Ave ☎ 253-3913

Longy School of Music, 3. 27 Garden St ☎ 876-0956

New School of Music, 1. 25 Lowell St ☎ 492-8105

Sanders Theater/Harvard, 4. Quincy St ☎ 496-2222

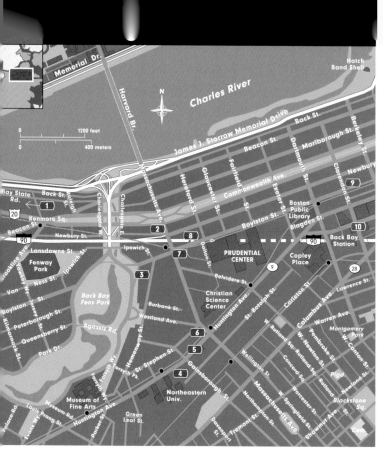

Listed by Site Number

1 Tsai Ctr/Boston Univ

2 Boston Children's Theatre

3 Boston Conservatory Theater

4 Boston Chamber Music Society

4 Jordan Hall/NE Conservatory

5 Huntington Theatre Co

6 Boston Pops

6 Boston Symphony

6 Handel & Haydn Soc

6 Symphony Hall

7 Berklee Perf Center

8 ICA Theater

9 Copley Theatre

10 Boston Camerata

10 Lyric Stage

Listed Alphabetically

Berklee Performance Ctr, 7.
136 Mass Ave ☎ 266-7455

Boston Ballet, 14. Wang Ctr,
270 Tremont St☎ 695-6950

Boston Camerata, 10.
140 Clarendon St ☎ 262-2092

Boston Center for the Arts (BCA), 12.
539 Tremont St ☎ 426-5000

Boston Chamber Music Society, 4.
Jordan Hall ☎ 349-0086

Boston Children's Theatre, 2.
93 Mass Ave ☎ 424-6634

Boston Conservatory Theater, 3.
8 The Fenway ☎ 536-6340

Boston Lyric Opera, 17.
Emerson Majestic Theatre ☎ 542-4912

Boston Pops, 6.
Symphony Hall ☎ 266-1492

Boston Symphony Orchestra, 6.
Symphony Hall ☎ 266-2378

Charles Playhouse, 13.
74 Warrenton St ☎ 426-6912

City Stage Co, 11.
551 Tremont St ☎ 542-2291

Colonial Theatre, 18.
106 Boylston St ☎ 426-9366

Copley Theatre, 9.
225 Clarendon St ☎ 266-7262

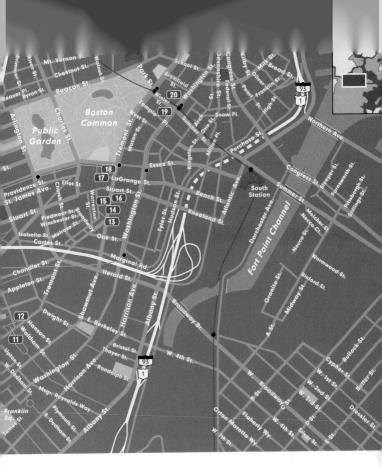

Listed by Site Number (cont.)

11 City Stage Company

12 Boston Center for the Arts

13 Charles Playhouse

14 Boston Ballet

14 Wang Center for the Performing Arts

15 Shubert Theatre

16 Wilbur Theatre

17 Dance Umbrella

17 Boston Lyric Opera

17 Emerson Majestic Theatre

18 Colonial Theatre

19 Walsh Theatre

20 Orpheum Theatre

Listed Alphabetically (cont.)

Dance Umbrella, 17. Emerson Majestic Theatre ☎ 482-7570

Emerson Majestic Theatre, 17. 219 Tremont St ☎ 824-8000

Handel & Haydn Society, 6. Symphony Hall ☎ 266-3605

Huntington Theatre Co, 5. 264 Huntington Ave ☎ 266-0800

Inst of Contemp Art Theater, 8. 955 Boylston St ☎ 266-5152

Jordan Hall/NE Conservatory, 4. 30 Gainsborough St ☎ 536-2412

Lyric Stage, 10. 140 Clarendon St ☎ 437-7172

Orpheum Theatre, 20. Hamilton Pl off Tremont St ☎ 679-0810

Shubert Theatre, 15. 265 Tremont St ☎ 482-9393

Symphony Hall, 6. 301 Mass Ave ☎ 266-1492

Tsai Performance Ctr/BU, 1. 685 Commonwealth Ave ☎ 353-8724

Wang Center for the Performing Arts, 14. 270 Tremont St ☎ 482-9393

Wilbur Theatre, 16. 246 Tremont St ☎ 423-4008

Walsh Theatre/Suffolk University, 19. 55 Temple St ☎ 573-8680

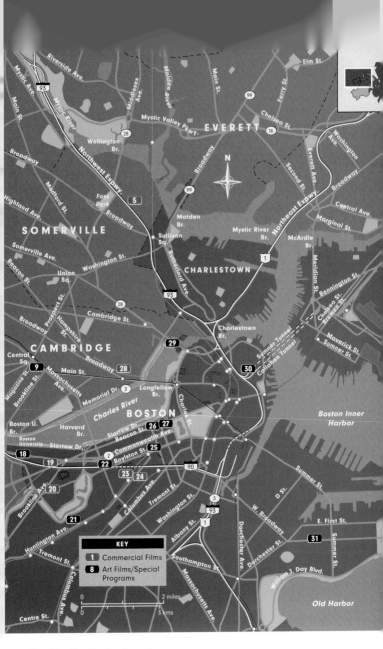

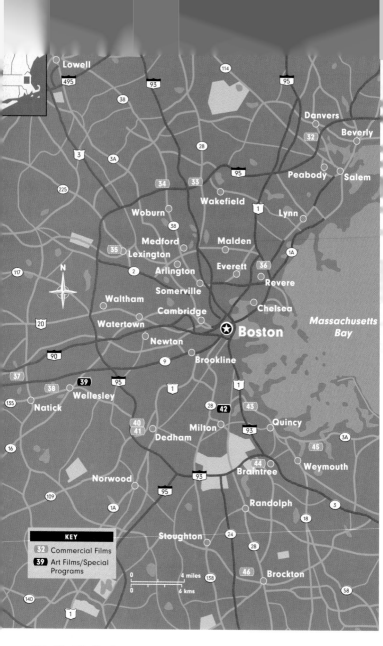

Massachusetts Bay

Boston

KEY

32 Commercial Films

39 Art Films/Special Programs

Listed Alphabetically

COMMERCIAL FILMS

Allston Cinemas, 15.
214 Harvard Ave ☎ 277-2140

Arlington Capitol Theater, 1.
204 Mass Ave ☎ 781/648-4340

Belmont Studio Cinema, 2.
376 Trapelo Rd ☎ 484-1706

Braintree 10, 44. off Forbes Rd
☎ 781/848-1070

Brattle Theater, 6. 40 Brattle St,
Cambridge ☎ 876-6837

Brockton Westgate 7, 46.
Rt 27 ☎ 508/588-5050

Burlington 10, 33. Rt 128, exit 32B
☎ 781/229-9200

Cheri, 23. 50 Dalton St
☎ 536-2870

Chestnut Hill General Cinema, 13.
27 Boylston St ☎ 277-2500

Cleveland Circle, 14. Cleveland
Circle, Brookline ☎ 566-4040

Coolidge Corner Cinema, 16.
Coolidge Cnr, Brookline ☎ 734-2500

Copley Place, 24.
100 Huntington Ave ☎ 266-1300

Danvers Liberty Tree Mall, 32. Rt
128, exit 4 ☎ 978/750-9019

Dedham Community Theatre, 40.
580 High St ☎ 781/326-1463

Dedham Showcase, 41. 950
Providence Hwy (Rt I)
☎ 781/326-4955

Fenway 13, 20. 201 Brookline Ave
☎ 333-3456

Framingham 14, 37.
Rt 9 ☎ 508/628-4404

Fresh Pond Cinema, 3. Fresh Pond
Plaza, Cambridge ☎ 661-2900

Harborlight Mall Cinema, 45.
Rt 3A, No Weymouth ☎ 781/337-5840

Harvard Square Theater, 7.
10 Church St, Cambridge ☎ 864-4580

Kendall Square Cinema, 28.
1 Kendall Sq, Cambridge ☎ 494-9800

Lexington Flick, 35.
1794 Mass Ave ☎ 781/861-6161

Natick Loews/Sony, 39.
Rt 9 ☎ 508/653-5005

Nickelodeon Loews/Sony, 19.
606 Commonwealth Ave ☎ 424-1500

Quincy Showcase, 43.
1585 Hancock St ☎ 773-5700

Revere Showcase, 36.
Rt I & Squire Rd ☎ 781/286-1660

Somerville Theater, 4.
55 Davis Sq ☎ 625-5700

Somerville Loews/Sony, 5.
Assembly Sq Mall ☎ 628-7000

West Newton Cinema, 12.
1296 Washington St ☎ 964-6060

Woburn Showcase, 34.
Rts 128 & 38 ☎ 781/933-5330

ART FILMS/SPECIAL PROGRAMS

Boston Public Library, 25.
666 Boylston St ☎ 536-5400

Boston Univ/Sherman Union, 18.
771 Commonwealth Ave ☎ 353-2169

Brighton Branch Library, 11.
40 Academy Hill Rd ☎ 782-6032

Brookline Public Library, 17.
361 Washington St ☎ 730-2345

Central Square Library, 9.
45 Pearl St, Cambridge ☎ 349-4010

Codman Square Library, 42. 690
Washington St, Dorchester
☎ 436-8214

French Library, 27.
53 Marlborough St ☎ 266-4351

Goethe Institute, 26.
170 Beacon St ☎ 262-6050

Harvard Film Archive, 8.
24 Quincy St, Cambridge ☎ 495-4700

Institute of Contemporary Art, 22.
955 Boylston St ☎ 266-5152

Museum of Fine Arts, 21.
465 Huntington Ave ☎ 267-9300

Museum of Science, 29.
Science Park ☎ 723-2500

Newton Free Library, 10.
414 Centre St, Newton Ctr ☎ 552-7145

North End Branch Library, 30.
25 Parmenter St ☎ 227-8135

South Boston Branch Library, 31.
646 E Broadway ☎ 268-0180

Wellesley Free Library, 39.
530 Washington St ☎ 781/253-1610

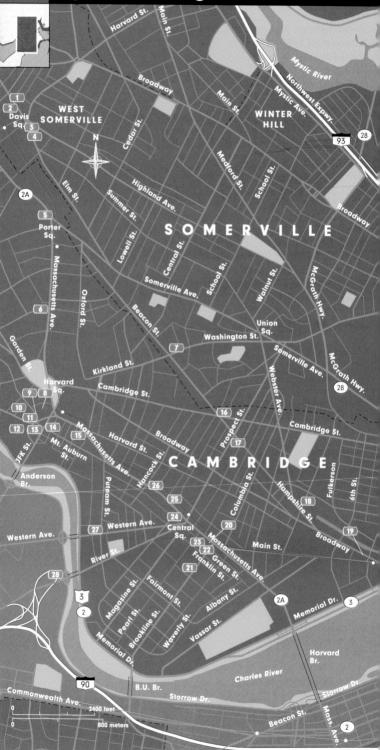

Harvard St.
Main St.
Mystic River
Broadway
Main St.
Mystic Ave.
Northwest Expwy.
WINTER HILL
Medford St.
Cedar St.
School St.
93
28
1
2
Davis Sq.
3
4
WEST SOMERVILLE
N
Elm St.
2A
Highland Ave.
Broadway
5
Porter Sq.
Summer St.
SOMERVILLE
McGrath Hwy.
Massachusetts Ave.
Oxford St.
Lowell St.
Central St.
School St.
Walnut St.
6
Somerville Ave.
Beacon St.
Union Sq.
Washington St.
Somerville Ave.
McGrath Hwy.
28
7
Webster Ave.
Garden St.
Kirkland St.
Cambridge St.
Cambridge St.
9 8
Harvard Sq.
16
Prospect St.
10
11
12 13 14
15
Massachusetts Ave.
Harvard St.
Broadway
17
JFK St.
Mt. Auburn St.
Hancock St.
CAMBRIDGE
Hampshire St.
Fulkerson
6th St.
26
18
Anderson Br.
Putnam St.
25
Columbia St.
19
Broadway
27
Western Ave.
24
20
Western Ave.
Central Sq.
Massachusetts Ave.
Main St.
River St.
23
2A
3
28
22
Green St.
Memorial Dr.
3
Franklin St.
Albany St.
2
21
Magazine St.
Pearl St.
Fairmont St.
Brookline St.
Waverly St.
Vassar St.
Memorial Dr.
Harvard Br.
Memorial Dr.
Charles River
Mass. Ave.
90
B.U. Br.
Storrow Dr.
Storrow Dr.
Commonwealth Ave.
2400 feet
Beacon St.
2
0
800 meters

Listed by Site Number

1 Johnny D's
2 Somerville Theater
3 Diesel Café
4 The Burren
5 Toad
6 Lizard Lounge
7 Kirkland Café
8 Passim
9 Brew Moon
10 Algiers Coffee House
11 Grendel's Den
12 Regattabar
13 House of Blues
14 John Harvard's Brew House
15 Comedy Studio
16 ImprovBoston
17 Ryles
18 Kendall Café
19 Cambridge Brewing Co
20 Phoenix Landing
21 ManRay
22 T.T. The Bear's
23 Middle East
24 Cantab Lounge/Third Rail
25 1369 Coffee House
26 Plough & Stars
27 Western Front
28 Scullers

Listed Alphabetically

Brew Moon, 9.
50 Church St, Cam
☎ 499-2739. Brewpub/DJ

Algiers Coffee House, 10.
40 Brattle St, Cam ☎ 492-1557.
Coffeehouse

The Burren, 4. 247 Elm St, Som
☎ 776-6896. Live Music/Folk Dancing

Cambridge Brewing Co, 19.
1 Kendall Square, Cam
☎ 494-1994. Live Music

Cantab Lounge/Third Rail, 24.
738 Mass Ave, Cam
☎ 354-2685. Live Music/Poetry

Comedy Studio, 15.
1236 Mass Ave, Cam
☎ 661-6507. Comedy

Diesel Café, 3. 257 Elm St, Som
☎ 629-8717. Coffeehouse

Grendel's Den, 11.
86 Winthrop St, Cam
☎ 491-1160. Bar

House of Blues, 13.
96 Winthrop St, Cam
☎ 491-2583. Live Blues

ImprovBoston, 16.
1253 Cambridge St, Cam
☎ 576-1253. Comedy

John Harvard's Brew House, 14.
33 Dunster St, Cam
☎ 868-3585. Live Music/Bar

Johnny D's, 1. 17 Holland St, Som
☎ 776-2004. Live Music

Kendall Café, 18. 233 Cardinal
Medeiros Way, Cam ☎ 661-0993.
Live Acoustic Music

Kirkland Café, 7. 425 Washington St,
Som ☎ 491-9640. Live Rock

Lizard Lounge, 6.
1667 Mass Ave, Cam
☎ 547-0759. Live Music/Poetry

ManRay, 21.
21 Brookline St, Cam
☎ 864-0400. Alternative

Middle East, 23.
472 Mass Ave, Cam
☎ 492-5162. Live Music

Passim, 8.
47 Palmer St, Cam
☎ 492-7679. Live Folk/Acoustic

Phoenix Landing, 20.
512 Mass Ave, Cam
☎ 576-6260. Live Music

Plough & Stars, 26.
912 Mass Ave, Cam
☎ 441-3455. Live Rock/Blues

Regattabar, 12.
Charles Hotel, Cam
☎ 876-7777. Live Jazz

Ryles, 17.
212 Hampshire St, Cam
☎ 876-9330. Live Jazz

Scullers, 28.
Doubletree Guest Suites,
400 Soldiers Field Rd, Allston
☎ 562-4111. Live Jazz

Somerville Theater, 2.
Davis Sq, Som
☎ 625-5700. Live Music

1369 Coffee House, 25.
757 Mass Ave, Cam
☎ 576-4600. Coffeehouse

Toad, 5.
1912 Mass Ave, Cam
☎ 497-4950. Live Music

T.T. The Bear's, 22.
10 Brookline St, Cam
☎ 492-2327. Live Music

Western Front, 27.
343 Western Ave, Cam
☎ 492-7772. Live Music

Kenmore Square & Lansdowne Street

Listed by Site Number

1	Harper's Ferry	**9**	Paradise	**16**	Clery's
2	Karma/Mambo Lnge	**10**	Other Side Cosmic Café	**17**	Delux Café & Lounge
3	Boston Beer Works	**11**	Milky Way Lounge	**18**	Club Café
4	Bill's Bar	**12**	Wally's Café	**19**	Ritz-Carlton Bar
5	Embassy/The Modern	**13**	Dick's Last Resort	**20**	Bull & Finch Pub
6	Axis	**13**	Top of the Hub	**21**	Jacque's
7	Avalon	**14**	Daisy Buchanan's	**22**	Vapor
8	Jillians	**15**	Turner Fisheries	**22**	Venu

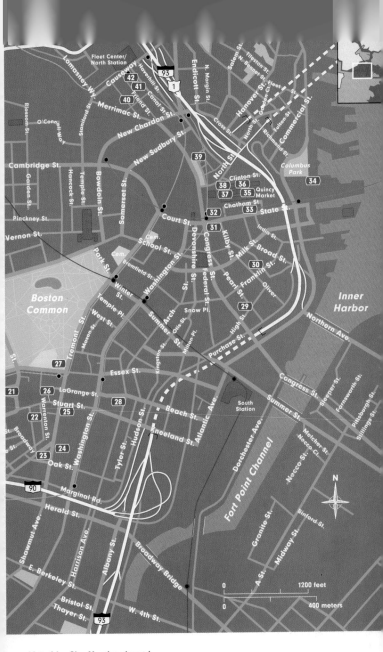

Listed by Site Number (cont.)

22 Nick's Comedy Stop	**29** International	**36** Atrium Lounge
23 NYC Jukebox	**30** Il Panino	**37** Comedy Connection
24 The Roxy	**31** Bay Tower Room	**38** Marketplace Cafe
25 Buzz/Club Europa	**32** Houlihan's	**39** Purple Shamrock
26 Brew Moon	**33** Waves	**40** Commonwealth Brewing Co
27 Dick Doherty's Comedy Vault	**33** Kitty O'Shea's	**41** Irish Embassy Pub
28 Les Zygomates	**34** Tia's	**42** Harp
	35 Black Rose	

Listed Alphabetically

Avalon, 7.
15 Lansdowne St ☎ 262-2424.
Dancing/Live Music

Atrium Lounge, 36.
Regal Bostonian, North & Blackstone
Sts ☎ 523-3600. Piano/Jazz/Cabaret

Axis, 6. 13 Lansdowne St
☎ 262-2437. Club/Varied Music

Bay Tower Room, 31.
60 State St ☎ 723-1666.
Dancing/Live Music

Bill's Bar, 4. 5½ Lansdowne St
☎ 421-9678. Bar/Live Music

Black Rose, 35. 160 State St
☎ 742-2286. Live Music

Boston Beer Works, 3.
61 Brookline Ave ☎ 536-2337.
Brewery

Brew Moon, 26. 115 Stuart St
☎ 523-6467. Brew Pub

Bull & Finch Pub, 20.
Hampshire House, 84 Beacon St
☎ 227-9605. Bar/Live Music

Buzz/Club Europa, 25.
51-67 Stuart St ☎ 267-8969.
Dancing/Gay/Straight

Clery's, 16.
113 Dartmouth St
☎ 262-9874. Live Music

Club Café, 18. 209 Columbus Ave
☎ 536-0966. Cabaret/Gay

Comedy Connection, 37.
Quincy Market ☎ 248-9700. Comedy

Commonwealth Brewing Co, 40.
138 Portland St ☎ 523-8383.
Brewery/Live Music

Daisy Buchanan's, 14.
240A Newbury St ☎ 247-8516. Bar/DJ

Delux Café & Lounge, 17.
100 Chandler St ☎ 338-5258. Bar

Dick Doherty's Comedy Vault, 27.
124 Boylston St ☎ 729-2565. Comedy

Dick's Last Resort, 13. 55 Huntington
Ave ☎ 267-8080. Live Music

Embassy/The Modern, 5. 36
Lansdowne St ☎ 536-2100. Live
Music

Harp, 42. 85 Causeway St
☎ 742-1010. Rock/Dancing

Harper's Ferry, 1. 158 Brighton Ave,
Allston ☎ 254-9743. Live Music

Houlihan's, 32. 60 State St
☎ 367-6377. Dancing/DJ

Il Panino, 30. 295 Franklin St
☎ 338-1000. Dancing

International, 29. 184 High St
☎ 542-4747. Dancing/DJ

Irish Embassy Pub, 41.
234 Friend St ☎ 742-6618. Live Music

Jacque's, 21. 79 Broadway
☎ 426-8902. Rock/Drag

Jillians, 8. 145 Ipswich St
☎ 437-0300. Pool/Billiards

Karma/Mambo Lounge, 2. 9
Lansdowne St ☎ 421-9595. Live Music

Kitty O'Shea's, 33. 131 State St
☎ 725-0100. Bar

Les Zygomates, 28. 129 South St
☎ 542-5108. Live Music

Marketplace Cafe, 38. Quincy
Market ☎ 227-9660. Live Music

Milky Way Lounge & Lanes, 11.
403 Centre St ☎ 524-3740. Live
Music/DJ/Dancing

Nick's Comedy Stop, 22. 100
Warrenton St ☎ 482-0930. Comedy

NYC Jukebox, 23. 275 Tremont St
☎ 542-4077. Dancing/DJ

Other Side Cosmic Café, 10.
407 Newbury St ☎ 536-9477.
Coffeehouse

Paradise, 9. 967 Commonwealth Ave
☎ 562-8820. Live Music

Purple Shamrock, 39. 1 Union St
☎ 227-2060. Bar/Varied Music

Ritz-Carlton Bar, 19.
15 Arlington St ☎ 536-5700. Bar

The Roxy, 24. 279 Tremont St
☎ 338-7699. Live Music/Dancing

Tia's, 34. Marriott Long Wharf
☎ 227-0828. Outdoor Bar

Top of the Hub, 13. Prudential
Center ☎ 536-1775. Bar

Turner Fisheries, 15.
Westin Hotel, 10 Huntington Ave
☎ 262-9600. Live Jazz

Vapor, 22. 100 Warrenton St
☎ 422-0862. Dancing/Gay

Venu, 22. 100 Warrenton St
☎ 338-8061. Dancing/DJ

Wally's Café, 12. 427 Mass Ave
☎ 424-1408. Jazz/Blues

Waves, 33. Marriott Long Wharf
☎ 227-0800. Dancing/DJ